Battle Orders • 5

OSPREY

M000240120

US Army in the Plains Indian Wars 1865–91

Clayton K S Chun • *Consultant editor Dr Duncan Anderson*

Series editors Marcus Cowper and Nikolai Bogdanovic

First published in Great Britain in 2004 by Osprey Publishing, Elms Court,
Chapel Way, Botley, Oxford OX2 9LP, United Kingdom.
Email: info@ospreypublishing.com

ISBN 1 84176 584 8

Editorial by Ilios Publishing, Oxford, UK (www.iliospublishing.com)
Design by Bounford.com, Royston, UK
Maps by Bounford.com, Royston, UK
Index by Alison Worthington
Originated by The Electronic Page Company, Cwmbran, UK
Printed and bound by L-Rex Printing Company Ltd

04 05 06 07 08   10 9 8 7 6 5 4 3 2 1

A CIP catalog record for this book is available from the British Library.

For a catalog of all books published by Osprey Military
and Aviation please contact:

Osprey Direct USA, c/o MBI Publishing, P.O. Box 1,
729 Prospect Ave, Osceola, WI 54020, USA
E-mail: info@ospreydirectusa.com

Osprey Direct UK, P.O. Box 140, Wellingborough,
Northants, NN8 2FA, UK
E-mail: info@ospreydirect.co.uk

www.ospreypublishing.com

Acknowledgments

I would like to express my thanks to Rich Baker, Jay Graybeal, and
Randy Hackenburg from the US Army Military History Institute,
who helped me with many research questions and with the
photographs for this book. Additionally, this book would not have
seen the light of day without the editorial support of Nikolai
Bogdanovic and Marcus Cowper at Ilios Publishing. Finally, I would
like to thank my family for their patience with me when
completing this work.

Photographic credits

All of the photographs that appear in this work are from the
archives of the US Army Military History Institute, Carlisle
Barracks, Pennsylvania. The collections of the Institute from which
they are taken are indicated at the end of each caption, together
with reference numbers.

Linear measurements

Distances, ranges, and dimensions are given in the
contemporary US system of inches, feet, yards, and
statute miles:

feet to meters:	multiply feet by 0.3058
yards to meters:	multiply yards by 0.9114
miles to kilometers:	multiply miles by 1.6093

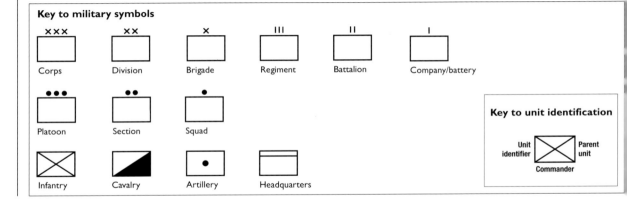

Key to military symbols

Corps / Division / Brigade / Regiment / Battalion / Company/battery

Platoon / Section / Squad

Infantry / Cavalry / Artillery / Headquarters

Key to unit identification

Unit identifier / Parent unit / Commander

Contents

Introduction

The United States was in a period of great transition during the late-spring of 1865. The nation had experienced and survived a bitter civil war and its leaders were desperately trying to bind together a divided country. Many sought a new beginning in the West, and a massive migration of emigrants rolled towards the Pacific. The railroad and civilization surged westward; not even geographical obstacles stopped this steady progress. Farmers and settlers at first encountered privation on the semi-arid plains, but the advance of the railroads and technology soon transformed the Plains into a livable area for emigrants.

However, the migration brought the white man into conflict with other peoples throughout the region: Native American Indian tribes. Although white and Indian conflicts had occurred in the past, the scale of this clash of civilizations reached continental proportions. The United States Army was one of the main protagonists. Army units stationed west of the Mississippi River both supported the development of the frontier and fought a range of engagements, from small actions that protected stage lines to major expeditions against hostile tribes. Soldiers also defended railroads and maintained order on newly established Indian reservations and agencies.

The main theater of conflict between 1865 and 1891 was the vast expanse of the Great Plains. This area lay in the heartland of the nation, an area that encompassed about one third of the continental United States, comprising the current states of North and South Dakota, Montana, Wyoming, Minnesota, Missouri, Iowa, Nebraska, Oklahoma, Kansas, portions of Colorado, sections of Texas, and parts of New Mexico. The fighting took place in dry, hot summers on the treeless and rolling grasslands, as well as in bitterly cold winters in the Rocky Mountains.

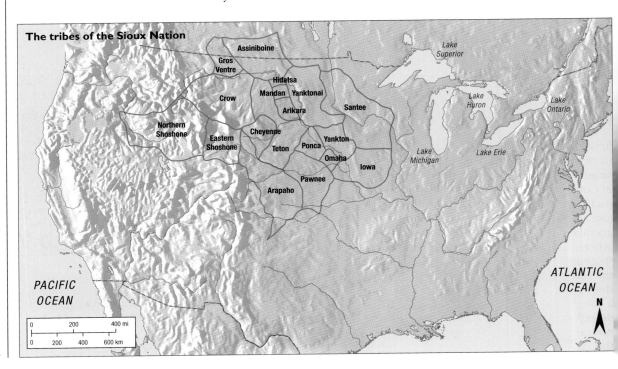

The tribes of the Sioux Nation

4

Approximately 270,000 Indians lived west of the Mississippi River in 1865. However, the Army had assigned only 15,417 soldiers to the whole of the Plains by 1867. Soldiers had to face a tough foe, rough territory, diverse tasks, and a penny-pinching government. They conducted combat operations with only surplus weapons and equipment, a factor that plagued the Army for years, as many officials and military officers on the War Department staff believed the real threat was from foreign invasion. The Indians might kill a few settlers or slow the development of the railroads, but they were no threat to the large eastern cities or to industrial production. The Army also focused its tactical attention on fighting massed armies, not small bands of Indians on horseback. Long distances and limited resources forced innovative officers to adapt to the challenges on the Plains.

For many people, the Little Big Horn campaign, where Army troops chased an elusive foe over hundreds of miles of rolling grasslands only to meet defeat, epitomizes the Plains Indian Wars. But this encounter was only one of many. Soldiers fought savage winter campaigns that ended in the destruction of Indian villages and encampments, such as the battles of the Washita in 1868 and Wounded Knee, which ended the conflict on the Plains during the winter of 1891. Smaller engagements involving only a few soldiers defending themselves or attempting to make an arrest on a reservation also occurred on the Plains: full-scale expeditions and campaigns became the exception rather than the rule. In reality, routine garrison duty in desolate locations marked the experience of most men.

The key trial faced by the Army was how to settle a country without the proper resources, direction, or organizational consensus. Army officers in the West had to rely on their professionalism, the adoption of new strategies, and other innovations. After the Civil War, and faced with an Indian threat once again, the Army had to alter its way of fighting with cavalry, infantry, and artillery. It found itself in the middle of variegated conflicts between Indians and a myriad of settlers; ranchers, outlaws, railroad crews, and others. While many Army officers advocated the annihilation of the Indians, others sympathized with the Native Americans' plight, but still obeyed orders to support the settlement of many Indian lands by white emigrants.

The Plains Indian Wars, like the Civil War, was a training ground for many junior and senior officers who would later form part of the nation's army in its first overseas conflict, the Spanish–American War. The Army conducted a series of operations during the Plains Indian Wars that would be echoed later in Cuba and the Philippines. Its soldiers faced hit-and-run ambushes, oversaw pacification programs, and evolved into a constabulary force. Army officers also adapted from fighting against a European-trained army to tackling a guerilla movement. The Wars reawakened the Army to forms of warfare that officers and men had not experienced for some years, and the value of flexibility, initiative, and innovation became more apparent to officers during the conflict. Successful officers adapted to a difficult environment by forcing their soldiers to apply appropriate and practical strategies and tactics against a tough, dedicated foe. Cavalry and infantry units had to be prepared to defend against and attack Sioux, Cheyenne, and other tribes at a moment's notice. Fortunately, for the Army, the officers and men on the Plains rose to this challenge well.

Active campaigning against hostile tribes was a tedious process that forced officers and men to leave the comfort of their posts for weeks. These officers from the 5th Cavalry are on campaign against the Sioux at French Creek in the Black Hills, Dakota Territory, during October 1876. (RG 262S Indian Wars Collection .77)

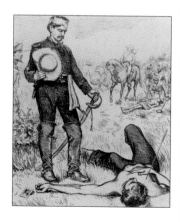

Reality on the Plains by Charles S. Reinhart represents a fanciful image of active service on the Plains. The victim's dying moments were spent gazing on the image of a loved one that has fallen from his left hand. (RG126 W.C. Brown .268)

Combat organization and mission

The United States Army used three main combat branches in the Plains Indian Wars: infantry, cavalry, and artillery. By far, the most common and numerous soldiers belonged to the infantry. Despite the movie and television stereotype of the cavalry's dashing appearance to save the day, the War Department officials valued the (cheaper) infantry more than they did the horse soldier. However, each branch had its advantages and disadvantages on the Plains and commanders learned to adjust to the particular operating characteristics of each.

Infantry

The infantry, for many years during the conflict, had more personnel and regiments than the cavalry and artillery combined. Infantry allowed a commander to operate on the undulating Plains, in mountains, and in all weather conditions. Infantrymen were also adaptable to fighting defensively or offensively and could perform their duty while entrenched or on the move.

The infantry provided Army commanders with mass firepower to strike the enemy, or break up an attack. Breech-loading rifles allowed soldiers to bring down massive, accurate fire that would devastate massed formations, although Indians did not fight with organized units. The effective range for breech-loading rifles was about 1,000 yards and officers considered a range of 500 yards "decisive" while that of 300 yards "annihilating" to the enemy. The bayonet charge was a rarity in the West and might not be necessary if the infantry could serve up sufficient fire.

Members of Congress and the War Department officials observed other benefits from the reliance on infantry. Infantry units could operate without costly support equipment. Cavalry relied for its mobility on expensive horses. Light artillery commanders not only required horses to pull caissons, but also required artillery pieces, whereas infantry soldiers only had small arms—relatively cheap weapons. The War Department could produce and maintain more infantry units, and these could operate with greater independence than the cavalry or artillery. Additionally, infantrymen did not require extensive logistical support.

Companies represented the mainstay of the Frontier Army. Small numbers and infrequent transfers allowed the officers and men to recognize the strengths and weaknesses of each member. This undated photograph shows Company K of the 1st Infantry Regiment. (RG 262S Indian Wars Collection .79)

These infantrymen at Fort Leavenworth, Kansas, c. 1884 symbolize the mainstay of the Army's presence in the West. The Department of the Missouri consistently had more infantry than cavalry units from 1865 to 1891. (RG24 Guy V. Henry .6)

The reliance on infantry did have several drawbacks though. The Army standard calculation of infantry mobility speeds was circa 2.5–2.75 miles per hour while a cavalry unit could walk at 4 miles per hour and gallop at 16 miles per hour. The infantry was slow to maneuver and move to battle. Infantry was also only effective up to the range of its rifles. Although infantry units could conduct most operations independently, they relied in part on the cavalry to screen them or provide reconnaissance. They also benefitted from the support of artillery units, which could produce high volumes of deadly, accurate cannon fire that might break up an attack or psychologically intimidate the Indian tribe or individual warrior.

The Sioux Indians called infantrymen "walk-a-heaps," reflecting the infantry's ability to move long distances in all weather conditions. The "walk-a-heaps," with their longer ranged, larger caliber rifles, had an advantage over the Indians, unless they came within range of their repeating rifles, arrows, or lances. Normally, infantry officers trained their men to fire as a prelude to a charge. Unfortunately, unless the Indians were in a defensive position or encamped, they simply rode away to avoid taking casualties. Also, limited ammunition or supplies on campaign often forced Army officers to guard against excessive rifle fire.

Cavalry

The Army employed its cavalry forces in four main ways. The commanding officer of a cavalry regiment or company could order his troops to conduct a shock action via a charge; to dismount for support or to independently attack the enemy; to fire when mounted; or to reconnoiter the area for the enemy.

The cavalry used shock actions to break up a concentrated enemy force, form the basis of a surprise attack, spearhead a counterattack, or conduct a breakthrough when surrounded. The cavalryman's primary weapon was the strength and size of his horse. The speed and rapid concentration of force produced the impact and shock of the attack. The saber, pistol, and carbine supplemented this.

In dismounted action, cavalrymen could produce disciplined fire or take advantage of their mobility to outflank an enemy and attack. Cavalry could act as an independent force, supplement infantry actions, or hold a position until relieved by other dismounted horse soldiers or infantry.

The cavalry could also provide disciplined fire while mounted, for example while acting as skirmishers or covering a fast moving retreat. However, while riding, the accuracy of such fire was questionable. Controlling a horse and firing while traversing broken ground might produce nothing more than intimidation of the enemy.

The 10th Cavalry served for years in the Division of the Missouri. Here they are shown on parade at Fort Custer, Montana. A typical regiment normally had about 840 officers and men in 1884. (RG100 B.F. Fiske .32)

Field organization for the US Army and its departmental locations, 1867. The Army's organization changed between 1860 and 1891. As Army units and the settlers moved westward, the conflict became more contained. The Army adapted its organization to reflect the anticipated threat to settlers, cities, and railroads.

Reconnaissance was the cavalry's most useful role. Such "detached action" provided intelligence; cavalry were the eyes and ears of a commander on expedition. Cavalrymen might act as a preemptive screen to surprise Indian ambushers or to discover the whereabouts of a camp in anticipation of an attack. Such cavalry detachments allowed the commander greater operational flexibility, offering scouting, reconnaissance, security, even small raiding forays.

Cavalry had a distinct advantage of mobility given the vast distances covered on the Plains. They could match the equally mobile Indians on ponies, and could rapidly deploy to places where military force was required. Surprise attacks or reconnaissance actions, although possible with slower infantry, were made much more effective as a result.

The Army was under no illusion that the cavalry was an expensive arm to fund. To effectively field a proper trooper required a horse, saddle, equipment support, and long training—costing three times as much as an ordinary infantryman. The relative efficiency of the cavalry versus the infantry was a topic of much debate during the conflict. Although the cavalry had a distinct advantage of speed and mobility, it required extensive logistical support for

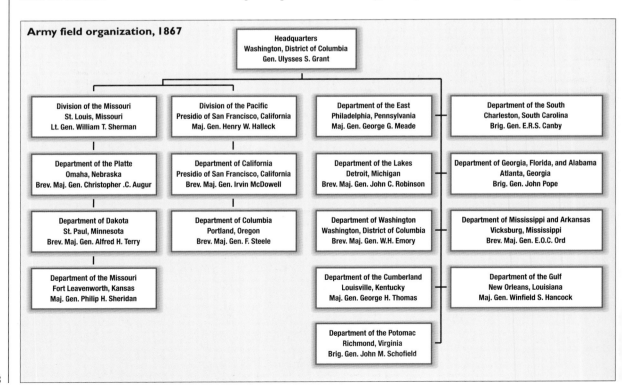

Army field organization, 1867

Headquarters
Washington, District of Columbia
Gen. Ulysses S. Grant

Division of the Missouri	Division of the Pacific	Department of the East	Department of the South
St. Louis, Missouri	Presidio of San Francisco, California	Philadelphia, Pennsylvania	Charleston, South Carolina
Lt. Gen. William T. Sherman	Maj. Gen. Henry W. Halleck	Maj. Gen. George G. Meade	Brig. Gen. E.R.S. Canby
Department of the Platte	**Department of California**	**Department of the Lakes**	**Department of Georgia, Florida, and Alabama**
Omaha, Nebraska	Presidio of San Francisco, California	Detroit, Michigan	Atlanta, Georgia
Brev. Maj. Gen. Christopher .C. Augur	Brev. Maj. Gen. Irvin McDowell	Brev. Maj. Gen. John C. Robinson	Brig. Gen. John Pope
Department of Dakota	**Department of Columbia**	**Department of Washington**	**Department of Mississippi and Arkansas**
St. Paul, Minnesota	Portland, Oregon	Washington, District of Columbia	Vicksburg, Mississippi
Brev. Maj. Gen. Alfred H. Terry	Brev. Maj. Gen. F. Steele	Brev. Maj. Gen. W.H. Emory	Brev. Maj. Gen. E.O.C. Ord
Department of the Missouri		**Department of the Cumberland**	**Department of the Gulf**
Fort Leavenworth, Kansas		Louisville, Kentucky	New Orleans, Louisiana
Maj. Gen. Philip H. Sheridan		Maj. Gen. George H. Thomas	Maj. Gen. Winfield S. Hancock
		Department of the Potomac	
		Richmond, Virginia	
		Brig. Gen. John M. Schofield	

items such as horse feed grain. In one instance, the 6th Infantry Regiment's commander, Col. William B. Hazen, noted: "After the fourth day's march of a mixed command, the horse does not march faster than the foot soldier, and after the seventh day, the foot soldier has to end his march earlier and earlier each day, to enable the cavalry to reach the camp the same day at all." Many infantrymen thought the cavalry was nothing more than lightly armed mounted infantry since they fought mostly in dismounted actions. The "walk-a-heaps" provided more firepower, and over a longer period could out-distance the cavalry. Cavalry officers believed their forces should attack when their targets were demoralized, of poor quality, exhausted, in retreat, unprepared, or under attack by infantry or artillery. Dismounted troops were best suited to reinforcing infantry in an emergency, filling a gap in a battle, and operating in wooded or broken terrain unsuited for mounted actions. Mounted troopers were best used when resisting small scouting or raiding parties, conducting a pursuit, covering a retreat, or slowing down an Indian mounted assault.

Troops E, F, H, J, and K from the 7th Cavalry and Troops D and L from the 5th Cavalry at Fort Sill in 1890. Fort Sill was home to many different regiments. (RG95 Fort Sill Collection Box 8)

Field organization for the US Army and its departmental locations, 1875.

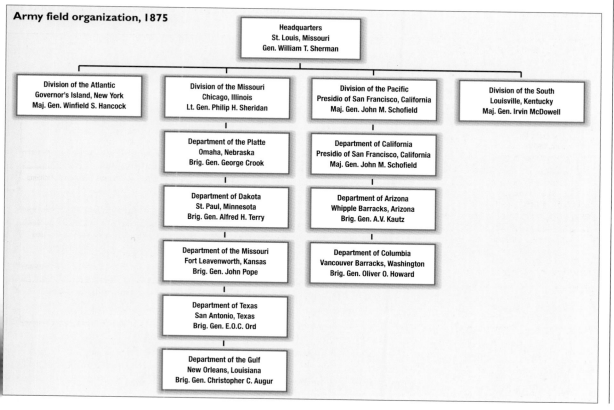

Army field organization, 1875

Headquarters
St. Louis, Missouri
Gen. William T. Sherman

Division of the Atlantic
Governor's Island, New York
Maj. Gen. Winfield S. Hancock

Division of the Missouri
Chicago, Illinois
Lt. Gen. Philip H. Sheridan

Division of the Pacific
Presidio of San Francisco, California
Maj. Gen. John M. Schofield

Division of the South
Louisville, Kentucky
Maj. Gen. Irvin McDowell

Department of the Platte
Omaha, Nebraska
Brig. Gen. George Crook

Department of California
Presidio of San Francisco, California
Maj. Gen. John M. Schofield

Department of Dakota
St. Paul, Minnesota
Brig. Gen. Alfred H. Terry

Department of Arizona
Whipple Barracks, Arizona
Brig. Gen. A.V. Kautz

Department of the Missouri
Fort Leavenworth, Kansas
Brig. Gen. John Pope

Department of Columbia
Vancouver Barracks, Washington
Brig. Gen. Oliver O. Howard

Department of Texas
San Antonio, Texas
Brig. Gen. E.O.C. Ord

Department of the Gulf
New Orleans, Louisiana
Brig. Gen. Christopher C. Augur

A captain commanded a cavalry troop (company), assisted by two lieutenants and several non-commissioned officers: the actual strength was frequently less than the authorized amount. (RG488 S.B. Young .66)

Artillery

The Army had two types of artillery units: heavy artillery batteries and light artillery companies. The role of the heavy batteries, with their large, immobile guns located in fortifications mainly on or near the coasts, was to defend the nation against raiders or amphibious invasion. Light artillery provided support to infantry and cavalry operations in the field. Horse-drawn caissons towed weapons, carried artillery crews, and delivered sufficient ammunition. The mobility of these units allowed them, in theory, to keep pace with the cavalry or infantry, and help defend against, or reinforce, offensive actions. Some companies were also armed as mountain artillery with mountain howitzers or guns of smaller caliber than horse-drawn cannons. These guns were designed to allow crews to assemble and disassemble them quickly. One piece could typically be carried by five pack-mules, with two mules transporting the gun and three moving the carriage and wheels.

Gatling guns and other rapid-fire weapons were also classified as artillery since their inventors intended the weapons to support the infantry or cavalry. For example, on April 7, 1875 near the Washita River, Lt. Col. Thomas H. Neill, commanding the 6th Cavalry, ordered his cavalry to charge 100–150 Cheyenne warriors holding positions on top of a hill—something not possible without covering fire. Neill ordered his Gatling gun to fire at 400 yards against the Cheyenne braves in support of combined cavalry and infantry charges.

Although artillery played a relatively minor role in the Plains Indian Wars, it did defend several key posts, and commanders took artillery on several key campaigns. The artillery's main purpose was to destroy enemy personnel or *matériel* from a distance. Since artillery crews could fire volleys of shells without the threat of receiving counter-fire, artillery seemed, at first, a weapon well suited to the Plains conflict. Additionally, if the artillery crews properly laid out fire, they avoided fighting in the "heat of battle," unlike the cavalry or infantry. Crews had the ability to direct artillery fire on a number of targets, unlike the infantry who concentrated their fire to their immediate front or rear. Artillery also severely intimidated Indians, with its long and accurate range, noise, and smoke.

The artillery had several weaknesses. Firstly, like cavalry, this branch of service was expensive to equip and maintain, with costly artillery pieces, horses, caissons, ammunition, and training. Secondly, even though light artillery was mobile, units had difficulty traversing the Plains or mountains on at best unimproved trails, or

as was more usually the case on rough terrain. Thirdly, light artillery supported infantry and cavalry and could not conduct independent operations. Fourthly, training required continuous practice and study, which was time consuming and demanding. Fifthly, the artillery's efficiency and effectiveness depended on the type of terrain and weather. Many of the major campaigns in the Plains Indian Wars were executed during the winter, aiming to catch the Indians unaware. Poor weather hindered aiming and distance calculations, while frozen ground affected the artillery's mobility.

When a commander employed artillery, fire would be directed against the enemy at the start of an engagement and continue as long as the enemy was on the field. Its value lay in how far it could achieve concentrated, accurate fire. Given the limited amount of ammunition and weapons taken on expedition, a wasteful projection of exploratory fire, such as shelling woods, was to be avoided at all costs.

Most Army posts had at least one artillery piece assigned, to support military operations. This Napoleon 12-pdr was located at Fort Missoula, Montana. (RG315 Daughters of the US Army .98)

The Army eventually replaced many of their Civil-War-era artillery pieces. These soldiers, shown in the field during the Pine Ridge campaign of 1890–91, have deployed with their 3.2in. breech-loading gun. (RG262S Indian Wars Collection .35)

Field organization

On campaign, Army commanders normally fielded a combined force of cavalry, infantry, and artillery. A large expeditionary force was usually composed of cavalry and infantry regiments, with perhaps a company or two of artillery. Officers used cavalry to locate, block, or attack the enemy at a distance from the main body. Once located, the expedition commander would use the infantry to provide considerable rifle fire. The Little Big Horn campaign, in the summer of 1876, provides a good illustration of a large-scale combined operation. About 3,500 uniformed personnel, more than 10 percent of the Army's strength, took part in this campaign against the Sioux. This was not a typical Plains engagement though: usually, the Army fielded only a company or two with a total strength of fewer than 100 officers and men.

The War Department did not significantly alter the character of the post-Civil War army until the 1890s. Army cavalry, infantry, and artillery units organized and fought against the Indians much the same way Civil War-era forces would have done. Although trained, armed and organized to fight against a massed opponent using similar weapons and tactics, the typical company commander soon learned that individual initiative was key.

The Army's mission and duties

The post-Civil War United States saw a tremendous population move towards the West. In the 1860s, about one million emigrants headed across the Plains; by the 1880s two and a half million settlers had traveled west. The lure of gold, land, ranching, and a new start in the territories sent a steady stream of settlers across the Plains and into conflict with the Native Americans. The Army's primary mission was to keep the peace between these settlers and the Indian population, to protect the western expansion of the nation, and to ensure that the tribes complied with various treaties. Its commanders faced a formidable task with few resources, inadequate support, the diversity of the terrain, extremes of weather, and the apathy of an uncaring public. A typical company

Field organization for the US Army and its departmental locations, 1884.

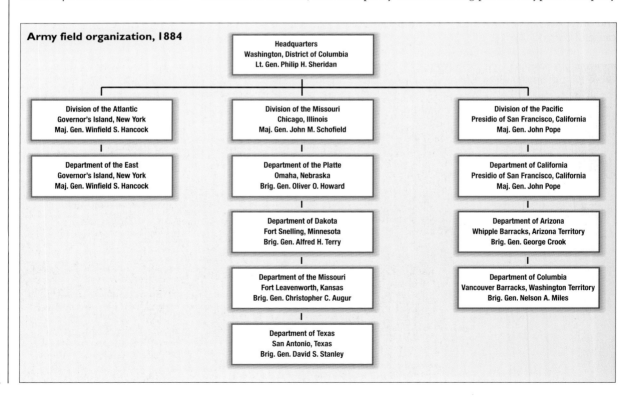

Army field organization, 1884

Headquarters
Washington, District of Columbia
Lt. Gen. Philip H. Sheridan

Division of the Atlantic
Governor's Island, New York
Maj. Gen. Winfield S. Hancock

Division of the Missouri
Chicago, Illinois
Maj. Gen. John M. Schofield

Division of the Pacific
Presidio of San Francisco, California
Maj. Gen. John Pope

Department of the East
Governor's Island, New York
Maj. Gen. Winfield S. Hancock

Department of the Platte
Omaha, Nebraska
Brig. Gen. Oliver O. Howard

Department of California
Presidio of San Francisco, California
Maj. Gen. John Pope

Department of Dakota
Fort Snelling, Minnesota
Brig. Gen. Alfred H. Terry

Department of Arizona
Whipple Barracks, Arizona Territory
Brig. Gen. George Crook

Department of the Missouri
Fort Leavenworth, Kansas
Brig. Gen. Christopher C. Augur

Department of Columbia
Vancouver Barracks, Washington Territory
Brig. Gen. Nelson A. Miles

Department of Texas
San Antonio, Texas
Brig. Gen. David S. Stanley

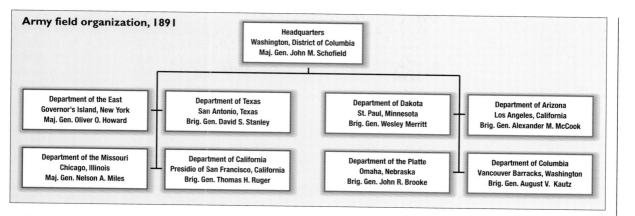

Army field organization, 1891

Headquarters Washington, District of Columbia Maj. Gen. John M. Schofield	

Department of the East Governor's Island, New York Maj. Gen. Oliver O. Howard	**Department of Texas** San Antonio, Texas Brig. Gen. David S. Stanley	**Department of Dakota** St. Paul, Minnesota Brig. Gen. Wesley Merritt	**Department of Arizona** Los Angeles, California Brig. Gen. Alexander M. McCook
Department of the Missouri Chicago, Illinois Maj. Gen. Nelson A. Miles	**Department of California** Presidio of San Francisco, California Brig. Gen. Thomas H. Ruger	**Department of the Platte** Omaha, Nebraska Brig. Gen. John R. Brooke	**Department of Columbia** Vancouver Barracks, Washington Brig. Gen. August V. Kautz

commander also had to deal with the fact that his subordinates were armed with weapons that arguably, had left them with less firepower than the Indians, and whose pay had been cut by Congress.

Many Army posts on the western prairies were in sight of the Indian reservations and could move to quell any uprisings. Their existence, in the heart of tribal lands, was a visible reminder of its potency. Additionally, the Army would use these bases to pacify new areas and advance further into hostile territory. Such action would restrict the movements of Indian warriors to an ever-shrinking but still significant area.

The Plains were dotted with small posts, manned by a single company. From these posts a company commander could maintain law and order, secure the area from threats posed by hostile Indians, and conduct operations and patrols. Cavalrymen and infantrymen were involved in untold disturbances throughout the Plains, often in a quest to find escaped Indians, make arrests of suspects for crimes, or other acts of law enforcement. Typical activities centered on post duties, such as constabulary actions, building roads, maintaining telegraph lines, and only occasionally stretched to fighting campaigns. Boredom was a common cause of complaint.

Field organization for the US Army, with departmental commanders and locations, 1891.

Army field expeditions required extensive logistical support, as demonstrated by the 1874 Black Hills expedition led by Lt. Col. George A. Custer and the 7th Cavalry. Note the artillery, cavalry flankers, and long wagon train. (RG126 W.C. Brown .148)

Doctrine and training

During the Civil War, Union and Confedereate army commanders relied on common doctrine. Both sides fought a predominantly conventional war that officers (educated at the United States Military Academy) were trained to execute against massed formations, a theory arising from the Napoleonic Wars where maneuver, mass, and firepower dominated. Similarly, citizen-soldier officers commanding volunteer units relied on drill manuals and regulations based upon European experience. Union and Confederate officers thus shared a mutual understanding of war. Frontier Army officers fighting the Plains Indian Wars, however, could not rely on established doctrine or training, and frequently had to improvise in the field. The United States government contributed to this confusion by advocating short-term and often confusing strategies.

Doctrine

Although settlers had been fighting against Indians since colonial times, few technical writers adopted lessons from these conflicts into official Army doctrine. Developing a formal doctrine that covered fighting from the plains to the mountains was difficult. The upper echelons of the Army's leadership also downplayed the importance of the Plains conflict, despite having the majority of Army forces assigned west of the Mississippi River. The real enemy (and thus the object of the doctrinal focus) was not perceived to be relatively small tribes of Indians, who could not threaten the nation's existence. Instead, military thought and theory concentrated on European countries that had the ability to invade and seize territory just as Great Britain had done in the War of 1812.

Regular Army officers, from those who commanded companies to those who directed the Army at the highest levels, were experienced Civil War veterans, and had put conventional warfare theory and doctrine into practice. From 1865 to 1891, a succession of high-level commanders, such as Ulysses S. Grant, William T. Sherman, Philip Sheridan, and John Schofield, faced a diverse military challenge from an enemy conducting widespread unconventional warfare. Professional officers found little glory in forcing errant tribes to return to a reservation or in patrolling vast prairie lands, and many were dispirited at the prospect of a Western

Marksmanship training was an important means to improving a soldier's effectiveness. Sgt. John Nihill, 5th Artillery, winner of the Congressional Medal of Honor, stands in the center of the third row in this 1887 photograph. (RG24 Guy V. Henry .40)

assignment. In addition, during the Civil War, the role of manning the frontier posts had fallen to volunteer (and not Regular Army) units—with the result that their experience in fighting the Indians departed with them when the Regular Army returned to the frontier at war's end.

These officers attempted to apply many of the doctrinal concepts from their experience and training to the Plains conflict. One of the most powerful concepts was the use of offensive action. Grant and Sherman had owed much of their Civil War fame to this: Grant's victories, albeit costly, in Virginia and Sherman's March to the Sea broke the back of the Confederacy. Similarly, the post-Civil War army could concentrate its meager resources striking blows against selected targets to force Indians back on to reservations or punish them for any transgressions.

One of the most famous concepts to evolve from this emphasis on the offensive was the use of converging columns. Army commanders fighting a mobile and elusive foe required considerable forces to find, deploy against, and engage the enemy. Unfortunately, the post-Civil War army had neither the structure nor sufficient detailed information to directly attack Indian tribes. Instead, Sheridan used offensive operations to concentrate his forces and entrap the enemy. The expeditionary force would use separate columns composed of cavalry or infantry to strike at a central target from different locations simultaneously. These converging columns created sufficient mass and shock to defeat an opponent. Sheridan was especially successful against the Southern Plains Indians and had largely eliminated this threat by the early-1870s.

The concept of converging columns did have several weaknesses. Commanders of undermanned posts had to relinquish what few soldiers they had for a campaign. This action left the defenses vulnerable to Indian attack or an emergency. Additionally, assembling an adequate force and coordinating movements took time. Regiments often had their companies assigned to geographically separated posts, but reformed for such campaigns. These companies had few opportunities to train together as a regiment, let alone fight as one. The relative lack of army mobility and logistical support also hampered operations: a major limiting constraint was the size and speed of the supply train, given that Army field units needed extensive food and equipment support. In addition, to be effective, converging columns required precise coordination to strike the enemy simultaneously, and also relied on the target being sizable and static. If one or more of these issues became a problem, the converging column approach could end in disaster, as happened to Custer's column at Little Big Horn.

The Army established few professional schools during the Plains Indian Wars. One exception was the US Infantry and Cavalry School. These members of the Class of 1885 would soon pass on their instruction to fellow officers in the field. (RG126 W.C. Brown .154)

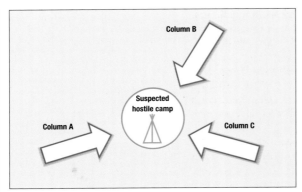

The concept of converging columns, shown in this diagram, was designed to encircle hostile Indian encampments.

One of the reasons the Army used converging columns was the mobility of the Indian tribes. If the Army could limit this, then the odds of a successful envelopment of the Indians increased greatly. Destroying or capturing pony herds became a prime objective. However, getting into position to eliminate pony herds was difficult. Sheridan proposed a more effective method. Unlike Army cavalry horses that subsisted on grain, Indian pony herds fed on grass. If the Army could attack during the winter, when the native grasses had withered, and the pony herds were weak from hunger, the tribes' mobility could be drastically reduced.

Winter warfare became an accepted operational procedure throughout the Plains Indian Wars. Indian tribes, with a lack of effective transport and hunting for support, tied themselves to encampments, making them relatively fixed targets. They normally constructed semi-permanent camps where there was a source of food, water, and wood, and a bluff or hill to shelter them from winter winds. Tribes were more focused on surviving the harsh winter than watching out for sudden attack. Braves were unlikely to leave their camps when under attack, and the cavalry or infantry could then kill or capture warriors, eliminate pony herds, destroy food supplies, and force any escaping Indians onto the frozen Plains.

Sheridan initiated the winter warfare concept on November 23, 1868 by sending Custer and his 7th Cavalry from Camp Supply, Oklahoma Territory, to attack Chief Black Kettle's village of Cheyenne Indians. Custer was able to find the village. A major advantage of winter warfare was the ability of Army guides or scouts to track Indian movements (and eventually their location) in the snow. Custer attacked the encampment, located on the Washita River, killed up to 105 Indians and captured 53 women and children. Many of the casualties were not warriors. Uncounted among the official dead were those who subsequently perished in the harsh winter retreat. Although Custer failed to consider other Indian villages on the Washita, Sheridan and Sherman regarded the attack as a great success. He had destroyed a herd of about 700 ponies, food supplies, and the camp, and forced Indian survivors to eventually return to the reservations. Sheridan's practice of destroying camps and starving the Indians into submission, tactics that he repeated throughout the Plains Indian Wars, were based on his experiences of destroying resources and weakening support for Confederate forces in the Shenandoah Valley in 1864.

The Army's concept of how to handle Indians also changed. Army leadership was unaccustomed to police actions and forcing tribes to return to the reservation. These commanders understood one type of struggle: total war. If the Army could destroy the resources and capabilities of errant Indian warriors, then it could dominate the Indians much as it did the Confederate Army by 1864. The Army sought a strategy to provide an overall direction to the problems in the West. Sherman and Sheridan provided one from their Civil War experiences that for many Indians proved all too successful.

Changing strategy

As settlers, the railroads, miners, and others moved with greater frequency through and onto lands ceded to the Indians, attacks occurred on both sides with great savagery. Army commanders found it increasingly difficult to provide protection to such a large influx of settlers. The lack of sufficient personnel, and calls for action from politicians, settlers, and inside the Army, forced a change in strategy.

The Army leadership continued the practice of operating posts throughout the West. However, newspapers began to report with increasing frequency

Indian "massacres" perpetuated on white settlers, railroad crews, and soldiers, which fueled demands for a more rapid solution to the Indian "problem." One such notable incident took place on December 21, 1866. Capt. William J. Fetterman, with 80 infantrymen, attempted to relieve a woodcutting party under attack from Fort Phil Kearney in present-day Wyoming. Fort Phil Kearney protected a portion of the Bozeman Trail, a direct entry into the goldfields of Montana. About 1,800 Sioux, Cheyenne, and Arapaho braves surrounded and attacked Fetterman's troops. None survived: their bodies were mutilated beyond recognition.

It was at this point that Lt. Gen. William T. Sherman, commander of the Division of the Missouri, moved the strategy of pacification into one of total war against "hostile" Indians. If an Indian tribe refused to return to a reservation or had committed a grievous act, then the Army conducted a "war of annihilation" against them. Military leaders pushed the offensive, as an operational concept, among departmental, regimental, and subordinate commands. Sherman stated to Grant, on December 28, 1868 that "We must act with vindictive earnestness against the Sioux, even to their extermination, men, women and children." In one sense, Sherman's statement can be intrepreted as frustration with a policy that limited his command to a static defensive posture, in which it suffered continual attacks. Sheridan also saw the war as total, but in contrast confined his strictures to combatants only. His orders to Custer before the campaign against Black Kettle on the Washita were simply to "Kill or hang all warriors and bring back all women and children." If soldiers could separate the warriors from the non-combatants in battle, then the strategy would eliminate Indian military capability. Unfortunately, when the Army conducted an attack on a village in winter with limited intelligence gathering, it frequently led to the slaughter of women and children.

Sherman turned to a strategy that used posts to secure territory, but also provided the ability to strike at any hostile Indian tribes, a practice that Sheridan continued. The Army needed to protect the burgeoning population and railroad system. As more white settlers explored previously undiscovered or desirable land, the emphasis on keeping Indian tribes on designated reservations became more marked. In short, the system allowed the government to keep Indian warriors under lock and key.

Regiments had few opportunities to operate and train as a unit. Still, officers attempted to prepare for campaigning, as demonstrated here at Fort Meade in the late-1880s. (RG113 M.F. Steele .101)

Rain-in–the-Face, a Sioux, poses here with a Winchester. These rapid-fire weapons gave some Indians a distinct firepower advantage over US Army soldiers. (RG485 E.S. Godfrey .309)

The reservation system was a method of dividing and weakening the tribes, and quashing any attempts to combine them. It allowed the Army to account for a tribe's location and removed any semblance of tribal independence. Army policy tried to ensure settlers and emigrants traveled unmolested; Indians had to stay within the confines of the reservation or the Army would swiftly punish any offenders. This policy worked well for smaller tribes.

Forcing some of the Indians to stay on the reservation was difficult given the appalling conditions there caused by a lack of suitable housing and food, and the trauma of cultural change. Longing to return to their old lifestyles, many tribes left the reservations. Some tribes would simply return to roam the Plains during the spring and summer and return to the reservation in the winter. Others left permanently. Whenever these tribes departed, the Bureau of Indian Affairs called in the Army to force their return or conduct a campaign against such "hostiles."

The US government's policies to solve the problems in the West revolved around political, economic, and military means. The Bureau of Indian Affairs, first under the War Department and later the Department of the Interior, limited tribal sovereignty and isolated each Indian nation. Individuals and tribes became dependent on government assistance as pressure from the development of the Plains limited their traditional land and food resources. The Army could select its targets for operations and often use brutal methods to quash any sign of resistance. However, the Bureau of Indian Affairs also controlled Army access to reservations, which limited its military options.

Army commanders who advanced the total war strategy pointed to its success in the Civil War. Fighting a strategy of annihilation against a unified Confederate force that was run, armed, and organized the same way seemed reasonable given the war's scope. Unfortunately, on the Plains the Indian tribes were not a homogeneous force. There was no single leader of Indian tribes. The main enemy of the Army on the Northern Plains was the Sioux nation, but this "nation" was composed of many tribes, some historical enemies. Likewise, on the Southern Plains, Kiowas, Comanches, and others were hardly a unified nation. Some tribes, like the Cheyenne, migrated nomadically across the Plains.

The Sioux comprised three major branches: the Tetons, Middle, and Eastern. The Tetons were further composed of Oglala, Brulé, Hunkpapa, Miniconju, Blackfoot, Sans Arc, and Two Kettle peoples. The Yanktons and Yanktonnais constituted the Middle branch. The Santee tribe made up the Eastern branch. These tribes did not usually act as a unified Sioux "nation" in terms of organizing or conducting raids. For many Sioux tribes, the main enemy was the Army. However, these tribes also conducted intertribal warfare. The name Sioux, freely translated, means "the enemy." They were not native to the Plains and had displaced Crow tribes from their Northern Plains homes during a period of western expansion. The Crows became "blood enemies" of the Tetons. During the Plains Indian Wars, the Crow, Arikara, Eastern Shoshone, and Pawnee became "allies" of the US government. Other tribes like the Yankton or Iowa merely accepted their fate and did not generally oppose the United States government. Crow and Arikara scouts served throughout the Army searching for and fighting against the Teton Sioux.

Braves conduct a Crow War Dance. (RG485 E.S. Godfrey .342)

Army commanders needed to modify their strategy in this respect, as the proper identification of friend or foe was critical. Frequently, Bureau of Indian Affairs agents might classify hostile tribes by their absence from a reservation, but the Army needed to avoid wasting precious resources on a winter campaign against friendly Indians.

Fighting a mobile foe also brought other considerations into play. The Army's strategy of annihilation would succeed if the Indians could be forced to face the Army in a decisive battle or the Army could use its relative resource superiority to grind the Indians into submission through attrition. The Indian tribes usually did not need to directly confront the Army. Separate tribal movements beyond the reservation or hit-and-run tactics forced the Army to spread its forces to protect settlements and other valuable assets. A mobile and careful enemy could avoid any slow-moving converging columns, particularly in summer. Most importantly, the could avoid a pitched battle—the objective of the Army's strategy—and its resulting heavy casualties.

The strategy became one of "selective totality." Few soldiers, reduced campaigning time, and the absence of fixed targets created a dilemma for commanders. Scattered engagements that included a sprinkling of hit-and-run attacks made major campaigns pointless. Instead, Army leaders continued to use outposts to gradually expand pacified areas, and increased the reach and control of the United States government. The pressure to submit to the reservation, or face starvation, forced tribal leaders to give up their independence. The Army then began to use its military superiority to eliminate any resistance thought to threaten the stability of the reservation system. Although not Army policy, the development of the Plains also contributed to the demise of tribal independence. Buffalo, one of the main food sources for the Plains Indians, was killed extensively for its hide and meat by white hunters. Without access to such sources of food, and under Army pressure, many tribes did succumb to the reservation system.

Training

The Army's training system to prepare soldiers for field service was inadequate. It concentrated on conventional warfare, seeing Indian warfare as merely a sideshow. Gen. Winfield S. Hancock, testifying before Congress in 1876, belittled the impact of Indian warfare on the Army. He categorically declared that this type of service was "entitled to no weight" while entertaining the Army's force structure, size, and organization. Preparation for combat would have to rely on a combination of individual leadership skills and veteran experience, and faith in the Army's superior resources. Despite these issues, the Army performed its mission.

Enlisted men

The typical enlisted recruit progressed from a recruit depot to small unit tactical training at his post assignment. In the early Plains Indian Wars period, recruits signed on to serve for three years for the infantry and five years for the cavalry. Later, enlisted terms changed to three years for all branches to entice more recruits. A recruit had to be at least 21 years old. The recruit depots provided an introduction to military life. Here they learned basic military formations, schedules and routines, worked fatigue details, and learnt discipline and obedience to orders. The recruit was toughened for field service with callisthenics and physical training programs. This process was the only systematic Army-wide training for new enlistees up to the 1880s.

The Army processed volunteers for military service at three main depots, depending on which branch of the Army a recruit joined. It ordered all future cavalrymen to Jefferson Barracks in Missouri, while new infantrymen and gunners traveled to David's Island, New York, or Columbus Barracks, Ohio. The induction lasted only three to four weeks and the recruit depot cadres came from line regiments that had served on the Plains or in other areas.

Army field commanders frequently complained about the lack of training of new personnel. A new enlistee later had their stay at the recruit depots extended from three to four months during the 1880s. This new training added marching by squad and company, the manual of arms, maintaining equipment other than small arms, and further recruit indoctrination. Trainers introduced potential cavalrymen to riding, mounted and dismounted saber and small arms drill, and marching. Although this training improved individual soldiering skills, they still needed tactical training to conduct field service.

After completion of recruit depot "training," the Army directed the soldier, as part of a replacement draft, to their post assignment. These drafts usually departed the depots via land-grant railroads. The United States government had helped finance the construction of the transcontinental rail system and the railroads were obliged to allow the Army access to travel free in some cases, or at a discounted fare. These drafts moved to the closest railhead and then moved on by wagon, boat, stage, or foot to their post. On one occasion, a draft marched about 600 miles from Corrine, Utah, to Helena, Montana.

Some new enlistees never entered recruit depots. Instead, these volunteers trained on the post where they signed their enlistment papers. These enlistees were at least aware of their area of operations and the local threats.

Once at their post, the new soldiers were supposed to receive further training in marksmanship and horsemanship. A recent arrival was frequently detailed to fatigue duty, guard mount, or construction projects. However, undermanned posts and constant deployments left few veterans to provide a comprehensive training program for the new soldier. The new soldier had to observe, learn, and apply fighting skills from these experienced veterans. On occasion, new draftees went immediately into field service.

Training for all soldiers throughout this period was constrained by Congressional thrift, as limited budgets affected military operations. For example, in 1872 the Army allocated only 90 rounds per soldier for annual marksmanship training—something that directly translated into poor field performance. By October 1877, Congress had raised the allotment to 240 rounds. Additionally, training time competed with routine post activities, such as kitchen detail.

Officers

Officers graduating from the United States Military Academy had orders to arrive directly at their units, where their commanders expected them to conduct operations from the time of their arrival. The Army would later develop advanced schools for artillery, infantry, and cavalry officers, but most of the training on Indian warfare came from veterans. Unit training was limited due to economy measures. Newly commissioned lieutenants from West Point constituted the majority of recent additions to the officer corps. Before the Civil War, most officers were West Point graduates. After the conflict, West Point graduates composed less than half of all commissioned officers, principally because volunteer militia officers and many civilians with Civil War commissions decided to continue their Army careers. The officer seniority system ensured that many of these officers would continue their service, even though few officers, other than West Point graduates, entered active duty.

Most West Point graduates found themselves assigned to the frontier. For example, the class of 1872 sent 96 percent of its graduates to the West. These officers had received four years of military training as part of their studies, but none of their instructors formally taught Indian warfare doctrine to them. Officers with recent frontier experience who served on the staff offered a limited insight into Indian warfare.

These Military Academy cadets received introductory training with artillery, cavalry, and infantry tactics during the course of their instruction. The Army expected cadets to learn sufficient skills to take the field immediately after graduation. (RG113 M.F. Steele .267)

The West Point cadet was educated to become an all-round leader. The curriculum attempted to produce an officer who would be an engineer, explorer, trainer, and soldier. Instructors expected cadets to master tactical drills based on battalion actions, not at company level, which is where most of the activity focused on the Plains. They demonstrated to future officers the firing of artillery, employment of cannon, and the manufacture of ammunition. Infantry training included how to teach soldiers to perform the manual of arms and the correct marching commands into battle. Cavalry instruction emphasized rudimentary horsemanship, drill, formations, and limited small arms training.

Military instruction at West Point concentrated on conventional warfare and how to execute basic maneuvers. Most of the drills centered on regimental actions, the main fighting units of the Civil War. Colonels normally commanded these units, while captains and lieutenants led companies. Lieutenants merely followed the instruction of the colonels with little ability to conduct independent operations. This training did not adequately prepare new lieutenants for the challenges of the Plains, where junior officers needed to make snap decisions without the guidance of senior officers.

Sherman did recognize the need to continue professional education in tactics for officers and wanted his officers to be made aware of the revolutions in military technology and warfare. Curiously, the motivation for this new concern was not from the frontier, but the Franco-Prussian War in 1870. He ordered the establishment of an Artillery School and Engineering School of Application in the 1870s, and the Army also founded the School of Application for Infantry and Cavalry at Fort Leavenworth, Kansas, in 1881. The instruction focused, again, on conventional warfare. Typically, the Army sent a lieutenant from a company to the appropriate school. He would later return to his company to instruct his fellow officers on the curriculum.

Unit organization

By the end of the Civil War in May 1865, the Union Army had reached a maximum strength of 1,000,516 uniformed personnel. By October 1, 1865, the government had returned more than 800,000 volunteers to civilian life, and the Army reverted to its pre-war structure. By mid-1866, the Regular Army was a mere shadow of itself, with an authorized strength of 30,000 soldiers. This force was tasked with overseeing the federal government's reconstruction programs in the South while guarding the frontiers, particularly the border with Mexico. However, Congress did respond to military needs by expanding the Army through the passage of the "Act to increase and fix the Military Establishment of the United States." President Andrew Johnson signed this into law on July 28, 1866 and the Army's size was allowed to rise to 54,302 soldiers.

The Army was, by this law, in better shape to ensure Congressional mandates concerning the post-war Reconstruction acts and protecting any

The major posts in the Division of the Missouri, 1867. Here, and in the maps on pages 34, 42, and 46, the modern state boundaries have been included to aid orientation.

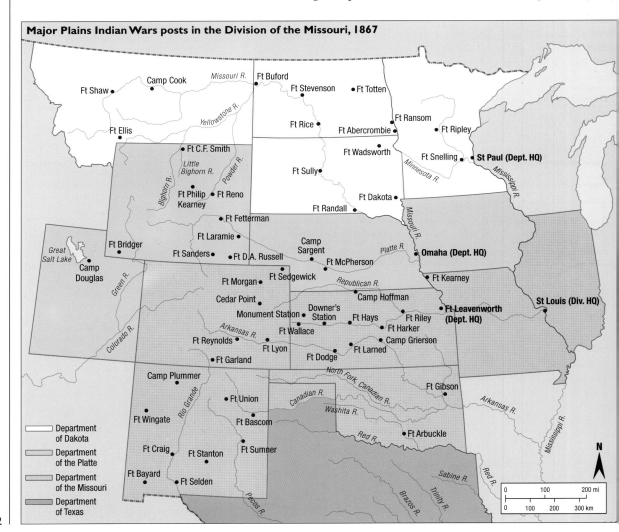

Major Plains Indian Wars posts in the Division of the Missouri, 1867

Department of Dakota
Department of the Platte
Department of the Missouri
Department of Texas

emigrants traveling west. Despite the structural increase, the Army was still faced with the task of guarding and conducting military operations over 2.5 million square miles from the Mississippi River to the Pacific Ocean. The posts created and manned to defend these territories fell under the authority of two geographic military divisions guided by the War Department.

The Army command and staff

The Army's higher command and staff functions had a curious relationship. Before the Civil War, a strict delineation of War Department responsibilities between the Secretary of War, a presidential appointee, and the Commanding General of the Army, a professional officer, was maintained. During the Civil War, the tension that existed between civilian and military control eased. The Commanding General of the Army was allowed more flexibility to conduct military operations and had greater freedom.

Ulysses S. Grant was General of the Armies and in supreme command of the Union Army. This distinction allowed him essentially to control all Army activities—operations and staff. Grant and Secretary of War Edwin M. Stanton had modified the system where Stanton's orders or direction were filtered through Grant. Grant continued this relationship and after his election to President, he ordered this subordination of the staff to continue. Unfortunately, Grant's Secretary of War, John A. Rawlins, convinced the President to reverse his decision and allow his office to directly issue orders throughout the Army. Several heads of these staff organizations "had grown to believe themselves not officers of the Army in the technical sense, but part of the War Department, the civil branch of the Government which connects the Army with the President

The Department of Dakota, 1867. The department formed part of the Division of the Missouri. In this diagram, and the others that follow in this chapter, each box contains the name of the post, the commanding officer, the units assigned, and reported strength.

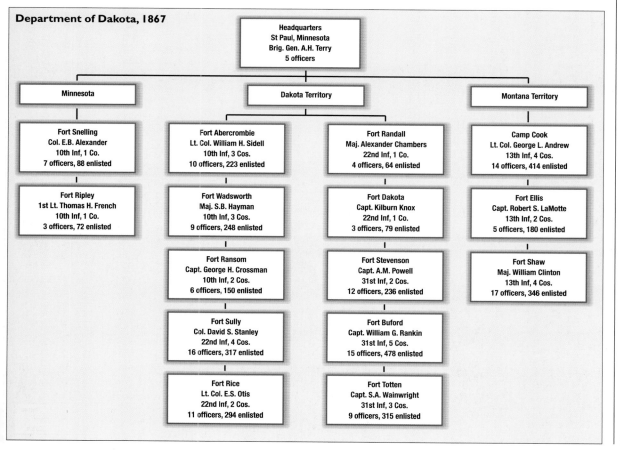

Department of Dakota, 1867

Headquarters
St Paul, Minnesota
Brig. Gen. A.H. Terry
5 officers

Minnesota

Fort Snelling
Col. E.B. Alexander
10th Inf, 1 Co.
7 officers, 88 enlisted

Fort Ripley
1st Lt. Thomas H. French
10th Inf, 1 Co.
3 officers, 72 enlisted

Dakota Territory

Fort Abercrombie
Lt. Col. William H. Sidell
10th Inf, 3 Cos.
10 officers, 223 enlisted

Fort Wadsworth
Maj. S.B. Hayman
10th Inf, 3 Cos.
9 officers, 248 enlisted

Fort Ransom
Capt. George H. Crossman
10th Inf, 2 Cos.
6 officers, 150 enlisted

Fort Sully
Col. David S. Stanley
22nd Inf, 4 Cos.
16 officers, 317 enlisted

Fort Rice
Lt. Col. E.S. Otis
22nd Inf, 2 Cos.
11 officers, 294 enlisted

Fort Randall
Maj. Alexander Chambers
22nd Inf, 1 Co.
4 officers, 64 enlisted

Fort Dakota
Capt. Kilburn Knox
22nd Inf, 1 Co.
3 officers, 79 enlisted

Fort Stevenson
Capt. A.M. Powell
31st Inf, 2 Cos.
12 officers, 236 enlisted

Fort Buford
Capt. William G. Rankin
31st Inf, 5 Cos.
15 officers, 478 enlisted

Fort Totten
Capt. S.A. Wainwright
31st Inf, 3 Cos.
9 officers, 315 enlisted

Montana Territory

Camp Cook
Lt. Col. George L. Andrew
13th Inf, 4 Cos.
14 officers, 414 enlisted

Fort Ellis
Capt. Robert S. LaMotte
13th Inf, 2 Cos.
5 officers, 180 enlisted

Fort Shaw
Maj. William Clinton
13th Inf, 4 Cos.
17 officers, 346 enlisted

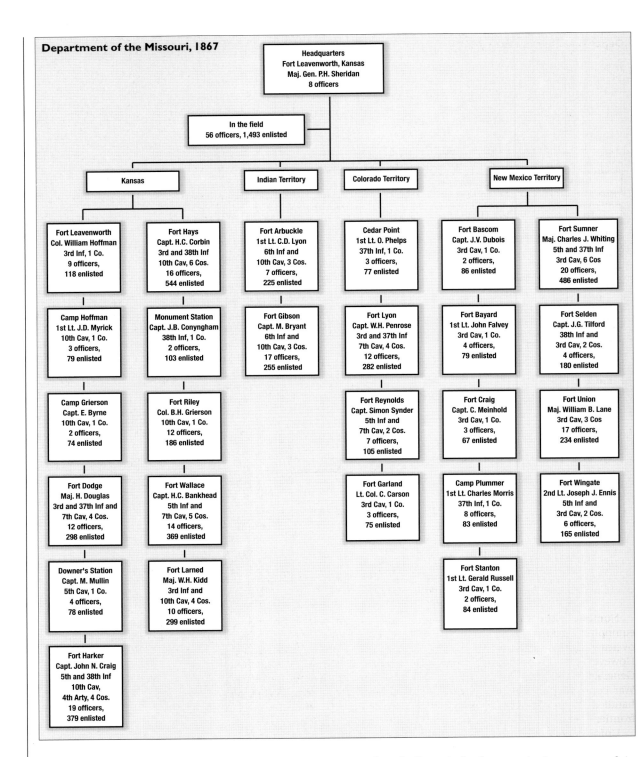

Department of the Missouri, 1867

Headquarters
Fort Leavenworth, Kansas
Maj. Gen. P.H. Sheridan
8 officers

In the field
56 officers, 1,493 enlisted

Kansas

Indian Territory

Colorado Territory

New Mexico Territory

Fort Leavenworth
Col. William Hoffman
3rd Inf, 1 Co.
9 officers,
118 enlisted

Fort Hays
Capt. H.C. Corbin
3rd and 38th Inf
10th Cav, 6 Cos.
16 officers,
544 enlisted

Fort Arbuckle
1st Lt. C.D. Lyon
6th Inf and
10th Cav, 3 Cos.
7 officers,
225 enlisted

Cedar Point
1st Lt. O. Phelps
37th Inf, 1 Co.
3 officers,
77 enlisted

Fort Bascom
Capt. J.V. Dubois
3rd Cav, 1 Co.
2 officers,
86 enlisted

Fort Sumner
Maj. Charles J. Whiting
5th and 37th Inf
3rd Cav, 6 Cos
20 officers,
486 enlisted

Camp Hoffman
1st Lt. J.D. Myrick
10th Cav, 1 Co.
3 officers,
79 enlisted

Monument Station
Capt. J.B. Conyngham
38th Inf, 1 Co.
2 officers,
103 enlisted

Fort Gibson
Capt. M. Bryant
6th Inf and
10th Cav, 3 Cos.
17 officers,
255 enlisted

Fort Lyon
Capt. W.H. Penrose
3rd and 37th Inf
7th Cav, 4 Cos.
12 officers,
282 enlisted

Fort Bayard
1st Lt. John Falvey
3rd Cav, 1 Co.
4 officers,
79 enlisted

Fort Selden
Capt. J.G. Tilford
38th Inf and
3rd Cav, 2 Cos.
4 officers,
180 enlisted

Camp Grierson
Capt. E. Byrne
10th Cav, 1 Co.
2 officers,
74 enlisted

Fort Riley
Col. B.H. Grierson
10th Cav, 1 Co.
12 officers,
186 enlisted

Fort Reynolds
Capt. Simon Synder
5th Inf and
7th Cav, 2 Cos.
7 officers,
105 enlisted

Fort Craig
Capt. C. Meinhold
3rd Cav, 1 Co.
3 officers,
67 enlisted

Fort Union
Maj. William B. Lane
3rd Cav, 3 Cos
17 officers,
234 enlisted

Fort Dodge
Maj. H. Douglas
3rd and 37th Inf and
7th Cav, 4 Cos.
12 officers,
298 enlisted

Fort Wallace
Capt. H.C. Bankhead
5th Inf and
7th Cav, 5 Cos.
14 officers,
369 enlisted

Fort Garland
Lt. Col. C. Carson
3rd Cav, 1 Co.
3 officers,
75 enlisted

Camp Plummer
1st Lt. Charles Morris
37th Inf, 1 Co.
8 officers,
83 enlisted

Fort Wingate
2nd Lt. Joseph J. Ennis
5th Inf and
3rd Cav, 2 Cos.
6 officers,
165 enlisted

Downer's Station
Capt. M. Mullin
5th Cav, 1 Co.
4 officers,
78 enlisted

Fort Larned
Maj. W.H. Kidd
3rd Inf and
10th Cav, 4 Cos.
10 officers,
299 enlisted

Fort Stanton
1st Lt. Gerald Russell
3rd Cav, 1 Co.
2 officers,
84 enlisted

Fort Harker
Capt. John N. Craig
5th and 38th Inf
10th Cav,
4th Arty, 4 Cos.
19 officers,
379 enlisted

Department of the Missouri, 1867, part of the Division of the Missouri. The department also maintained a small contingent at Jefferson Barracks, Missouri.

and Congress." Grant agreed and allowed the bureaus to become equal in status to the Commanding General. Sherman, who had succeeded Grant as Commanding General, was dumbstruck. Thus, in the period of the Plains Indian Wars, the command and staff functions of the Army were clouded by the resultant bureaucracy, something that ultimately affected the performance of field units.

Department of the Platte, 1867

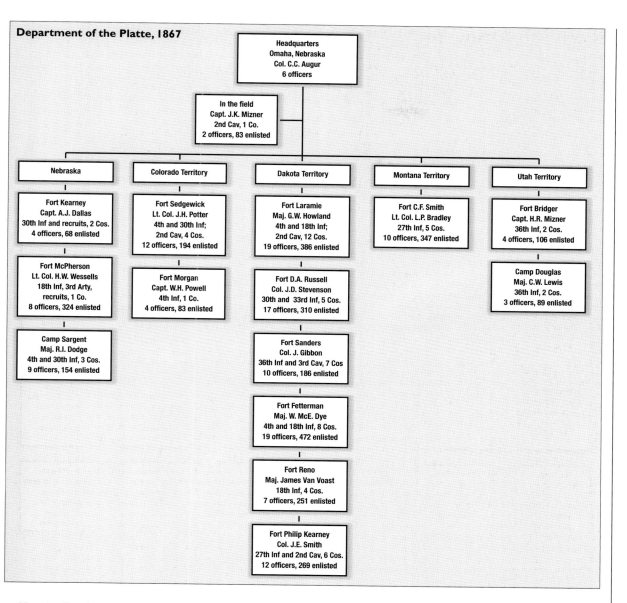

```
                          ┌─────────────────────┐
                          │    Headquarters     │
                          │   Omaha, Nebraska    │
                          │   Col. C.C. Augur    │
                          │     6 officers       │
                          └─────────────────────┘
                   ┌──────────────────────┐
                   │     In the field     │
                   │   Capt. J.K. Mizner   │
                   │    2nd Cav, 1 Co.    │
                   │ 2 officers, 83 enlisted │
                   └──────────────────────┘
```

Nebraska	Colorado Territory	Dakota Territory	Montana Territory	Utah Territory
Fort Kearney Capt. A.J. Dallas 30th Inf and recruits, 2 Cos. 4 officers, 68 enlisted	**Fort Sedgewick** Lt. Col. J.H. Potter 4th and 30th Inf; 2nd Cav, 4 Cos. 12 officers, 194 enlisted	**Fort Laramie** Maj. G.W. Howland 4th and 18th Inf; 2nd Cav, 12 Cos. 19 officers, 386 enlisted	**Fort C.F. Smith** Lt. Col. L.P. Bradley 27th Inf, 5 Cos. 10 officers, 347 enlisted	**Fort Bridger** Capt. H.R. Mizner 36th Inf, 2 Cos. 4 officers, 106 enlisted
Fort McPherson Lt. Col. H.W. Wessells 18th Inf, 3rd Arty, recruits, 1 Co. 8 officers, 324 enlisted	**Fort Morgan** Capt. W.H. Powell 4th Inf, 1 Co. 4 officers, 83 enlisted	**Fort D.A. Russell** Col. J.D. Stevenson 30th and 33rd Inf, 5 Cos. 17 officers, 310 enlisted		**Camp Douglas** Maj. C.W. Lewis 36th Inf, 2 Cos. 3 officers, 89 enlisted
Camp Sargent Maj. R.I. Dodge 4th and 30th Inf, 3 Cos. 9 officers, 154 enlisted		**Fort Sanders** Col. J. Gibbon 36th Inf and 3rd Cav, 7 Cos 10 officers, 186 enlisted		
		Fort Fetterman Maj. W. McE. Dye 4th and 18th Inf, 8 Cos. 19 officers, 472 enlisted		
		Fort Reno Maj. James Van Voast 18th Inf, 4 Cos. 7 officers, 251 enlisted		
		Fort Philip Kearney Col. J.E. Smith 27th Inf and 2nd Cav, 6 Cos. 12 officers, 269 enlisted		

Nominally, the Secretary of War was responsible for organizing, training, equipping the Army, plus the conduct of its operations. Additionally, Congress oversaw certain activities, from the supply of ammunition to training. However, the tension between previous Secretaries of War and Commanding Generals of the Army rose to the surface once more. By law, the Secretary of War controlled all staff and fiscal matters while the Commanding General handled all military activities. Fiscal matters could have an obvious impact on frontier operations though, by limiting supplies, transportation, or pay.

Unfortunately, the Army's clear chain of command from the Commanding General of the Army to a private on the frontier did not include its extensive staff functions. The War Department contained ten separate administrative or support bureaus that provided specific functional support to the whole army, comprising the Adjutant General, Inspector General, Judge Advocate General, Quartermaster, Subsistence, Medical, Pay, Ordnance, Signal, and Corps of Engineers. These bureaus, unfortunately, were independent of the Commanding General of the Army (see the diagram on page 26). The Army

The Department of the Platte, 1867, another constituent part of the Division of the Missouri.

staff controlled activities that directly supported field operations, as well as others beyond the control of the division or department commanders.

As Commanding General of the Army, Sherman believed that he could not effectively or efficiently fight any Western campaign, let alone protect settlers. Vital supplies, under the Quartermaster, might not reach field units in time or sufficient quantity to fight a campaign. The Ordnance staff might not produce or acquire weapons that particular commanders needed. Sherman did not receive information from the bureaus, nor was he consulted to coordinate actions. He had to rely on lower echelon divisional or departmental reports for details of support granted to field units.

The relation between Rawlins' successor as Secretary of War, William W. Belknap, and Sherman rapidly deteriorated. Sherman decided to move his headquarters from Washington, DC to St Louis, Missouri, in October 1874, declaring that he could not run the Army from Washington. He frequently protested that he learned more about the Army from newspaper accounts than from the War Department. Curiously, Belknap had served under Sherman as a division commander in the Civil War. Belknap was convinced that the military needed to be firmly under civilian control and he believed he could directly issue orders to the field without Sherman's concurrence. Sherman's failure to obtain information from the Secretary and the War Department staffs was a point of great frustration. He believed the Army could not operate effectively because of the Secretary of War's capacity to send orders to field and support units without informing the Commanding General of the Army. This problem was only resolved when Belknap was forced to resign as Secretary: he was accused of selling franchises authorizing traders to act as post sutlers, who sold goods to soldiers, their families, and Indians. The Democratic-controlled Congress wanted to embarrass the Republican Grant and pushed for Belknap's immediate impeachment.

The Army chain of command in 1872. The personnel figures indicate authorized strength.

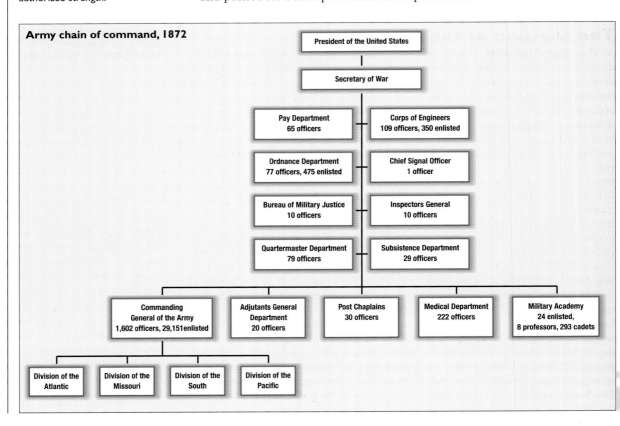

Army chain of command, 1872

President of the United States

Secretary of War

Pay Department 65 officers	Corps of Engineers 109 officers, 350 enlisted
Ordnance Department 77 officers, 475 enlisted	Chief Signal Officer 1 officer
Bureau of Military Justice 10 officers	Inspectors General 10 officers
Quartermaster Department 79 officers	Subsistence Department 29 officers

Commanding General of the Army 1,602 officers, 29,151 enlisted

Adjutants General Department 20 officers

Post Chaplains 30 officers

Medical Department 222 officers

Military Academy 24 enlisted, 8 professors, 293 cadets

Division of the Atlantic

Division of the Missouri

Division of the South

Division of the Pacific

Following Belknap's resignation, Sherman returned to Washington in 1876. Sherman was allowed to control military activities and issue orders to the field. Control over the staff bureaus was not resolved until 1903.

The Army maintained military discipline wherever it deployed its companies. This 1887 award ceremony at Bellevue, Nebraska, demonstrates the pride and professionalism of the Army on the Plains. (RG24 Guy V. Henry .38)

The Division of the Missouri

At the end of the Civil War, the United States Army was administratively divided into geographical military divisions. By 1872 these comprised the divisions of the Atlantic, Missouri, Pacific and the South. The divisions of the Atlantic and the South had very little contact with Indians, and instead occupied themselves with Reconstruction Act sanctioned activities, labor disputes, and protecting the nation's coastal areas from invasion. The divisions of the Pacific and Missouri bore the brunt of the Indian conflicts, and the western posts and their assigned units fell under one of these two commands, which were roughly separated by the Rocky Mountains. These divisions provided administrative support. For example, Sherman, as commander of the Division of the Missouri, ensured that any support for summer emigrant wagon trains was coordinated throughout the command to offer travelers protection throughout the Plains. Division headquarters also designed, planned, and organized military campaigns. The division commander had to provide overall policy and guidance, and a strategic direction for his command. He was also responsible for implementing administrative directives and orders from the War Department and Commanding General of the Army.

Within the division, communications were difficult, with posts spread thinly over hundreds of miles. Compounding this were jurisdictional questions between divisions. The mobile nature of the Plains Indians created situations where campaigns or engagements might straddle divisional or internal departmental lines. Additionally, divisional commanders had to deal with the Bureau of Indian Affairs, which was responsible for operating the reservation system that fed, clothed and housed the Indians, and reporting on tribal activities. The Bureau could call for the support of the Army to quell reservation unrest or demand the return of roaming Indians to reservations. Local commanders not

Large military campaigns required the Army to concentrate its regiments before deployment. George Crook formed his military camp in Wyoming before the start of the Little Big Horn campaign in summer 1876. (RG315 Daughters of the US Army .355)

only supported reservation authorities, but also state governors, local officials, the railroads, stage lines, farmers, ranchers, and others.

The Military Division of the Pacific, with its main headquarters at the Presidio of San Francisco, was composed of three military departments: Arizona, California, and Columbia. The Division of the Pacific dealt with several Indian uprisings including the Apaches in Arizona, Modocs in California, Nez Percé, Paiute, and other tribes. The Division also was tasked with settling labor disputes and manning coastal fortifications.

The Plains Indian Wars were mostly fought within the jurisdiction of the Division of the Missouri. Sioux tribes heavily populated its territory, but other tribes like the Cheyenne, Comanche, and Kiowa also occupied the Division's attention. These tribes created the most serious opposition to westward expansion, and as a result, most of the Army's resources supported operations in this division. The Division's command was originally located at St Louis, but it later moved to Chicago, Illinois.

The Division comprised several departments, and much of the heavy Indian fighting occurred on the Northern Plains. The Department of Dakota encompassed the area of modern-day Minnesota, North Dakota, and parts of South Dakota and Montana, and the Commanding General of this

Open barracks in permanent quarters were typical of the frontier during the late-1880s. These soldiers are part of Company H, 18th Infantry at Fort Riley, Kansas in 1887. (RG 262 Indian Wars Collection .262)

Permanent posts multiplied throughout the West, as the army replaced temporary installations with better, more stable ones. This unidentified post in 1883 illustrates the emphasis on better facilities. (RG488 S.B. Young .73)

department directed activities from St Paul, Minnesota. The department not only protected several overland trails, but the Northern Pacific railroad routes that ran through the territory. The department commander was no armchair general. He frequently joined units on active campaign. For example, Brig. Gen. Alfred H. Terry led a column against the Sioux during the 1876 Little Big Horn campaign, which included Custer's 7th Cavalry.

The other departments within the Division of the Missouri were the Platte, Missouri, and Texas. The Department of the Gulf's jurisdiction alternated between the Division of the Missouri and the Division of the Atlantic. The Department of the Gulf included units stationed in Arkansas, Louisiana, Mississippi, and Alabama.

The Department of the Platte was created in March 1866 to protect and assist in the construction of another vital railroad system, the transcontinental Union Pacific. The Department oversaw Army operations throughout Iowa, Nebraska, Wyoming, Utah, and portions of the Dakotas and Montana. Additionally, several key overland trails that enabled hundreds of thousands of settlers to cross the Plains (such as the Bozeman, California, and Oregon trails) originated within or passed through the Platte's boundaries. The Department's headquarters were located in Omaha, Nebraska. The Department of the Missouri contained the

Besides active campaigning and fatigue details, Army officers ensured that standards were maintained by conducting regular troop reviews, as demonstrated here by the 7th Cavalry at Fort Riley, Kansas. (RG485 E.S. Godfrey .365)

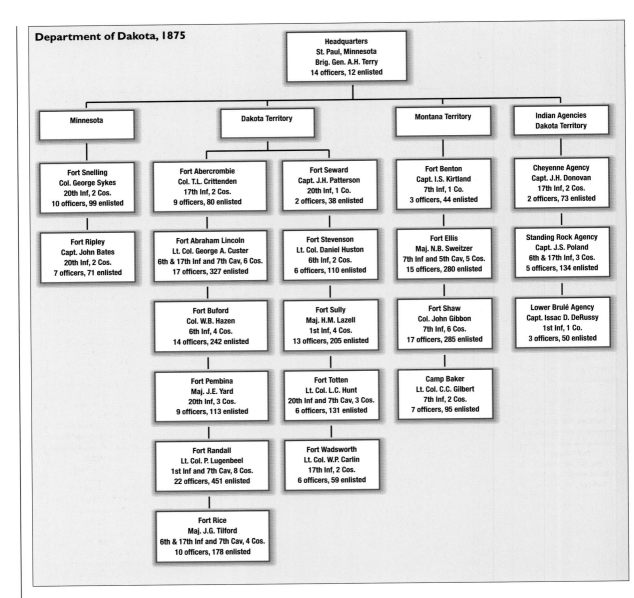

Department of Dakota, 1875

Headquarters
St. Paul, Minnesota
Brig. Gen. A.H. Terry
14 officers, 12 enlisted

Minnesota

Dakota Territory

Montana Territory

Indian Agencies
Dakota Territory

Fort Snelling
Col. George Sykes
20th Inf, 2 Cos.
10 officers, 99 enlisted

Fort Abercrombie
Col. T.L. Crittenden
17th Inf, 2 Cos.
9 officers, 80 enlisted

Fort Seward
Capt. J.H. Patterson
20th Inf, 1 Co.
2 officers, 38 enlisted

Fort Benton
Capt. I.S. Kirtland
7th Inf, 1 Co.
3 officers, 44 enlisted

Cheyenne Agency
Capt. J.H. Donovan
17th Inf, 2 Cos.
2 officers, 73 enlisted

Fort Ripley
Capt. John Bates
20th Inf, 2 Cos.
7 officers, 71 enlisted

Fort Abraham Lincoln
Lt. Col. George A. Custer
6th & 17th Inf and 7th Cav, 6 Cos.
17 officers, 327 enlisted

Fort Stevenson
Lt. Col. Daniel Huston
6th Inf, 2 Cos.
6 officers, 110 enlisted

Fort Ellis
Maj. N.B. Sweitzer
7th Inf and 5th Cav, 5 Cos.
15 officers, 280 enlisted

Standing Rock Agency
Capt. J.S. Poland
6th & 17th Inf, 3 Cos.
5 officers, 134 enlisted

Fort Buford
Col. W.B. Hazen
6th Inf, 4 Cos.
14 officers, 242 enlisted

Fort Sully
Maj. H.M. Lazell
1st Inf, 4 Cos.
13 officers, 205 enlisted

Fort Shaw
Col. John Gibbon
7th Inf, 6 Cos.
17 officers, 285 enlisted

Lower Brulé Agency
Capt. Issac D. DeRussy
1st Inf, 1 Co.
3 officers, 50 enlisted

Fort Pembina
Maj. J.E. Yard
20th Inf, 3 Cos.
9 officers, 113 enlisted

Fort Totten
Lt. Col. L.C. Hunt
20th Inf and 7th Cav, 3 Cos.
6 officers, 131 enlisted

Camp Baker
Lt. Col. C.C. Gilbert
7th Inf, 2 Cos.
7 officers, 95 enlisted

Fort Randall
Lt. Col. P. Lugenbeel
1st Inf and 7th Cav, 8 Cos.
22 officers, 451 enlisted

Fort Wadsworth
Lt. Col. W.P. Carlin
17th Inf, 2 Cos.
6 officers, 59 enlisted

Fort Rice
Maj. J.G. Tilford
6th & 17th Inf and 7th Cav, 4 Cos.
10 officers, 178 enlisted

southern reaches of the Plains. The Department included all of present-day Missouri, Kansas, Colorado, and New Mexico, and parts of Oklahoma and Texas. Its Commanding General supervised and administrated Army actions from Fort Leavenworth, Kansas. This department also contained the important Kansas Pacific rail line linking St Louis to Denver. The department also protected several overland trails to southern California and Arizona. The commander of the Department of Texas directed Army activities throughout most of Texas and portions of Oklahoma from his headquarters in San Antonio, Texas.

By 1876, the Military Divisions were commanded by a major-general and the departments normally overseen by a brigadier-general. The divisional staffs had a bare minimum of personnel, comprising a military secretary, three aide-de-camps, an Adjutant General's Office representative, two Inspector General Office personnel, four members each from the Quartermaster and Subsistence departments, a Medical Department officer, one Ordnance Department member, a Corps of Engineers staff officer, and twelve enlisted soldiers. The departmental staff closely mirrored the divisional one. The

Department of the Missouri, 1875

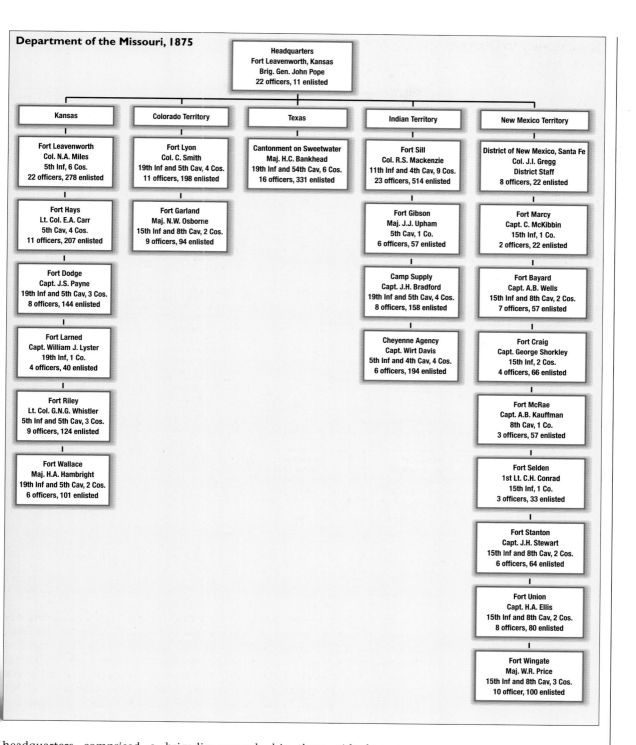

Headquarters
Fort Leavenworth, Kansas
Brig. Gen. John Pope
22 officers, 11 enlisted

Kansas

Fort Leavenworth
Col. N.A. Miles
5th Inf, 6 Cos.
22 officers, 278 enlisted

Fort Hays
Lt. Col. E.A. Carr
5th Cav, 4 Cos.
11 officers, 207 enlisted

Fort Dodge
Capt. J.S. Payne
19th Inf and 5th Cav, 3 Cos.
8 officers, 144 enlisted

Fort Larned
Capt. William J. Lyster
19th Inf, 1 Co.
4 officers, 40 enlisted

Fort Riley
Lt. Col. G.N.G. Whistler
5th Inf and 5th Cav, 3 Cos.
9 officers, 124 enlisted

Fort Wallace
Maj. H.A. Hambright
19th Inf and 5th Cav, 2 Cos.
6 officers, 101 enlisted

Colorado Territory

Fort Lyon
Col. C. Smith
19th Inf and 5th Cav, 4 Cos.
11 officers, 198 enlisted

Fort Garland
Maj. N.W. Osborne
15th Inf and 8th Cav, 2 Cos.
9 officers, 94 enlisted

Texas

Cantonment on Sweetwater
Maj. H.C. Bankhead
19th Inf and 54th Cav, 6 Cos.
16 officers, 331 enlisted

Indian Territory

Fort Sill
Col. R.S. Mackenzie
11th Inf and 4th Cav, 9 Cos.
23 officers, 514 enlisted

Fort Gibson
Maj. J.J. Upham
5th Cav, 1 Co.
6 officers, 57 enlisted

Camp Supply
Capt. J.H. Bradford
19th Inf and 5th Cav, 4 Cos.
8 officers, 158 enlisted

Cheyenne Agency
Capt. Wirt Davis
5th Inf and 4th Cav, 4 Cos.
6 officers, 194 enlisted

New Mexico Territory

District of New Mexico, Santa Fe
Col. J.I. Gregg
District Staff
8 officers, 22 enlisted

Fort Marcy
Capt. C. McKibbin
15th Inf, 1 Co.
2 officers, 22 enlisted

Fort Bayard
Capt. A.B. Wells
15th Inf and 8th Cav, 2 Cos.
7 officers, 57 enlisted

Fort Craig
Capt. George Shorkley
15th Inf, 2 Cos.
4 officers, 66 enlisted

Fort McRae
Capt. A.B. Kauffman
8th Cav, 1 Co.
3 officers, 57 enlisted

Fort Selden
1st Lt. C.H. Conrad
15th Inf, 1 Co.
3 officers, 33 enlisted

Fort Stanton
Capt. J.H. Stewart
15th Inf and 8th Cav, 2 Cos.
6 officers, 64 enlisted

Fort Union
Capt. H.A. Ellis
15th Inf and 8th Cav, 2 Cos.
8 officers, 80 enlisted

Fort Wingate
Maj. W.R. Price
15th Inf and 8th Cav, 3 Cos.
10 officer, 100 enlisted

headquarters comprised a brigadier-general, his three aide-de-camps, representatives from the Adjutant General's Office, Bureau of Military Justice, Corps of Engineers, Ordnance Department, two members from the Quartermaster and Subsistence departments, a military storekeeper, six representatives from the Pay Department, and eleven enlisted men. Some of the larger departments were further broken down into geographic districts that provided administrative and logistical support to dispersed posts.

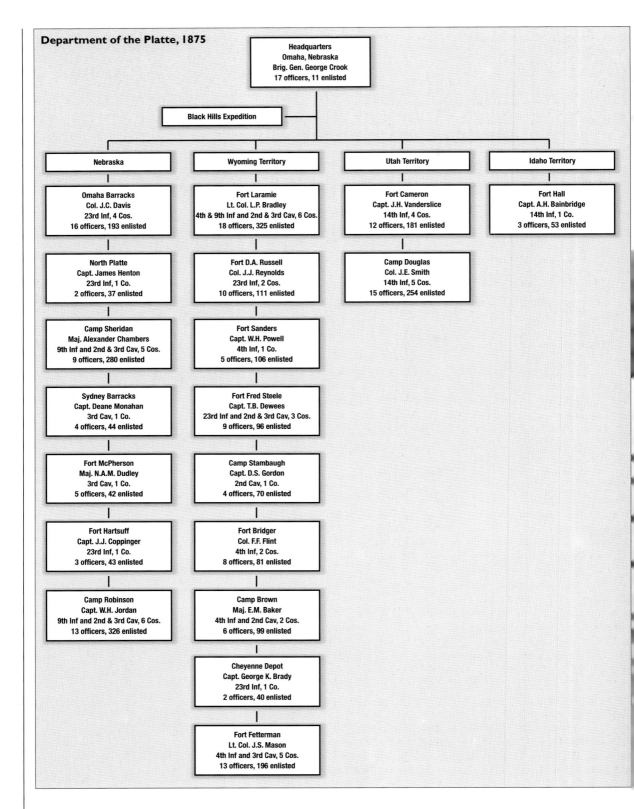

Department of the Platte, 1875

Headquarters
Omaha, Nebraska
Brig. Gen. George Crook
17 officers, 11 enlisted

Black Hills Expedition

Nebraska

Omaha Barracks
Col. J.C. Davis
23rd Inf, 4 Cos.
16 officers, 193 enlisted

North Platte
Capt. James Henton
23rd Inf, 1 Co.
2 officers, 37 enlisted

Camp Sheridan
Maj. Alexander Chambers
9th Inf and 2nd & 3rd Cav, 5 Cos.
9 officers, 280 enlisted

Sydney Barracks
Capt. Deane Monahan
3rd Cav, 1 Co.
4 officers, 44 enlisted

Fort McPherson
Maj. N.A.M. Dudley
3rd Cav, 1 Co.
5 officers, 42 enlisted

Fort Hartsuff
Capt. J.J. Coppinger
23rd Inf, 1 Co.
3 officers, 43 enlisted

Camp Robinson
Capt. W.H. Jordan
9th Inf and 2nd & 3rd Cav, 6 Cos.
13 officers, 326 enlisted

Wyoming Territory

Fort Laramie
Lt. Col. L.P. Bradley
4th & 9th Inf and 2nd & 3rd Cav, 6 Cos.
18 officers, 325 enlisted

Fort D.A. Russell
Col. J.J. Reynolds
23rd Inf, 2 Cos.
10 officers, 111 enlisted

Fort Sanders
Capt. W.H. Powell
4th Inf, 1 Co.
5 officers, 106 enlisted

Fort Fred Steele
Capt. T.B. Dewees
23rd Inf and 2nd & 3rd Cav, 3 Cos.
9 officers, 96 enlisted

Camp Stambaugh
Capt. D.S. Gordon
2nd Cav, 1 Co.
4 officers, 70 enlisted

Fort Bridger
Col. F.F. Flint
4th Inf, 2 Cos.
8 officers, 81 enlisted

Camp Brown
Maj. E.M. Baker
4th Inf and 2nd Cav, 2 Cos.
6 officers, 99 enlisted

Cheyenne Depot
Capt. George K. Brady
23rd Inf, 1 Co.
2 officers, 40 enlisted

Fort Fetterman
Lt. Col. J.S. Mason
4th Inf and 3rd Cav, 5 Cos.
13 officers, 196 enlisted

Utah Territory

Fort Cameron
Capt. J.H. Vanderslice
14th Inf, 4 Cos.
12 officers, 181 enlisted

Camp Douglas
Col. J.E. Smith
14th Inf, 5 Cos.
15 officers, 254 enlisted

Idaho Territory

Fort Hall
Capt. A.H. Bainbridge
14th Inf, 1 Co.
3 officers, 53 enlisted

Department of the Platte, 1875. Col. R.I. Dodge's expedition into the Black Hills had a strength of eight companies from the 2nd and 3rd Cavalry, with elements from the 9th Infantry.

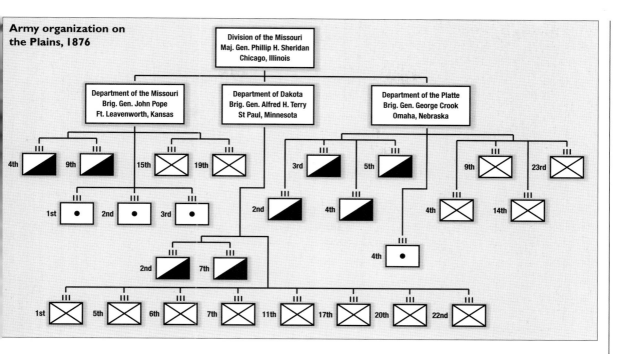

Army organization on the Plains, 1876

The vast majority of soldiers were sent to the Military Division's regiments. However, some divisional personnel were allocated to duties that did not directly support combat operations or assignments in the field. Officers and men were also detailed to a number of functions outside their division, such as running recruit depots, supporting the War Department staff and Washington bureaus, serving tours of duty as faculty or staff at West Point, or being detached to special duties.

The regiments

The Army's regimental system comprised a relatively small number of regular infantry, artillery, and cavalry units. Many of the regiments had long histories and established traditions, and veterans may have survived duty before and during the Civil War. Fewer soldiers and an expanding role to the west of the Mississippi and to the south of the Mason–Dixon Line required regiments to spread themselves thinly throughout the country.

Several Army reorganization acts, prior to 1870, first added to then merged regiments, before reducing the number of standing ones. In 1866, the Army's size increased, changing its organizational structure. The Regular Army was authorized to recruit and maintain more personnel, from its pre-war strength, of 19 infantry regiments to 45 such units. Similarly, the cavalry was increased from six to ten regiments. The total number of artillery regiments remained at only five though. The Commanding General of the Army was also allowed to maintain 1,000 Indian scouts. The Army was also granted the permanent creation of two regular African-American cavalry and four African-American infantry regiments. Such units had proven their combat capability in the Civil War and were used throughout the West to fight Indians and build the frontier. In addition, four infantry regiments of the Veteran Reserve Corps were authorized. These regiments were composed of Union soldiers who had been wounded in the Civil War and were not medically fit for active campaigning, but who could serve garrison duty. As a result, those units relieved of garrison duty could provide other services on the frontier for divisional commanders.

On March 3, 1869, in a cost-saving move Congress decided to reduce the size of the Army from 54,302 to 37,313 officers and men. Regiments were eliminated

Army organization on the Plains, 1876, showing the units and detachments assigned to the departments. The Division of the Missouri also included the departments of Texas and the Gulf. Some regiments had companies in different departments, and the Little Big Horn expedition forced the temporary assignment of units in the Department of the Platte to the Department of the Dakota.

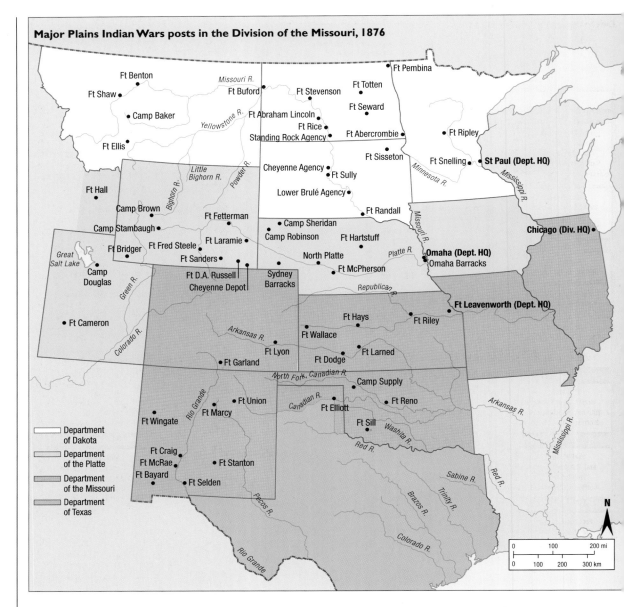

Major Plains Indian Wars posts in the Division of the Missouri, 1876

Ft Benton
Ft Shaw
Camp Baker
Ft Ellis
Missouri R.
Ft Buford
Ft Stevenson
Ft Pembina
Ft Totten
Ft Seward
Yellowstone R.
Ft Abraham Lincoln
Ft Rice
Standing Rock Agency
Ft Abercrombie
Ft Ripley
Ft Sisseton
Ft Snelling
St Paul (Dept. HQ)
Little Bighorn R.
Cheyenne Agency
Ft Sully
Minnesota R.
Ft Hall
Powder R.
Bighorn R.
Lower Brulé Agency
Mississippi R.
Camp Brown
Ft Fetterman
Ft Randall
Camp Stambaugh
Camp Sheridan
Camp Robinson
Ft Hartstuff
Chicago (Div. HQ)
Ft Bridger
Ft Fred Steele
Ft Laramie
Missouri R.
Great Salt Lake
Ft Sanders
North Platte
Platte R.
Omaha (Dept. HQ)
Camp Douglas
Ft D.A. Russell
Cheyenne Depot
Sydney Barracks
Ft McPherson
Omaha Barracks
Green R.
Ft Cameron
Republican R.
Ft Leavenworth (Dept. HQ)
Colorado R.
Arkansas R.
Ft Hays
Ft Riley
Ft Wallace
Ft Lyon
Ft Dodge
Ft Larned
Ft Garland
North Fork, Canadian R.
Camp Supply
Rio Grande
Ft Union
Ft Marcy
Canadian R.
Ft Elliott
Ft Reno
Arkansas R.
Ft Wingate
Ft Sill
Washita R.
Ft Craig
Ft McRae
Ft Stanton
Red R.
Ft Bayard
Ft Selden
Pecos R.
Sabine R.
Red R.
Brazos R.
Trinity R.
Mississippi R.
Rio Grande
Colorado R.

N

Department of Dakota
Department of the Platte
Department of the Missouri
Department of Texas

0   100   200 mi
0   100   200   300 km

or merged into new ones: many soldiers complained about the changes. The total number of infantry regiments was reduced to 25, the Veteran Reserve Corps was eliminated, and the four African-American infantry regiments were reorganized into two regiments.

In July 1870, the total number of enlisted soldiers was limited to 30,000 personnel. Further cuts in 1874 reduced the number of enlisted soldiers to 25,000 for a total strength of some 27,000 officers and men. This size of force served the Army throughout most of the Plains Indian Wars, up to the Spanish American War in 1898.

A typical Regular Army regiment had a small administrative headquarters whose staff mirrored the divisional and departmental ones in terms of function and size. A full colonel normally commanded the regiment with a lieutenant colonel as an assistant. A cavalry regimental staff had three majors, an adjutant (usually a lieutenant), one quartermaster officer, a single commissary officer, two veterinary surgeons (one commissioned), a sergeant major, quartermaster

Department of the Missouri, 1876

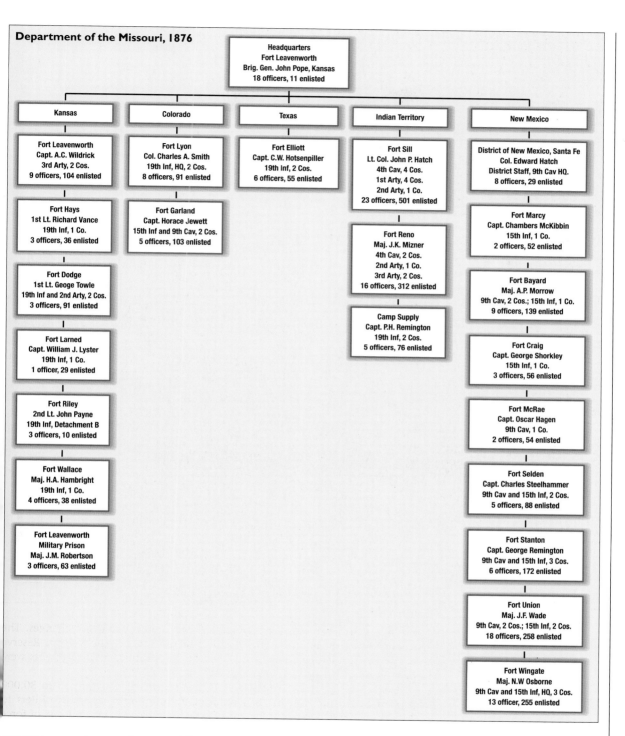

Headquarters
Fort Leavenworth
Brig. Gen. John Pope, Kansas
18 officers, 11 enlisted

Kansas

Fort Leavenworth
Capt. A.C. Wildrick
3rd Arty, 2 Cos.
9 officers, 104 enlisted

Fort Hays
1st Lt. Richard Vance
19th Inf, 1 Co.
3 officers, 36 enlisted

Fort Dodge
1st Lt. Geoge Towle
19th Inf and 2nd Arty, 2 Cos.
3 officers, 91 enlisted

Fort Larned
Capt. William J. Lyster
19th Inf, 1 Co.
1 officer, 29 enlisted

Fort Riley
2nd Lt. John Payne
19th Inf, Detachment B
3 officers, 10 enlisted

Fort Wallace
Maj. H.A. Hambright
19th Inf, 1 Co.
4 officers, 38 enlisted

Fort Leavenworth
Military Prison
Maj. J.M. Robertson
3 officers, 63 enlisted

Colorado

Fort Lyon
Col. Charles A. Smith
19th Inf, HQ, 2 Cos.
8 officers, 91 enlisted

Fort Garland
Capt. Horace Jewett
15th Inf and 9th Cav, 2 Cos.
5 officers, 103 enlisted

Texas

Fort Elliott
Capt. C.W. Hotsenpiller
19th Inf, 2 Cos.
6 officers, 55 enlisted

Indian Territory

Fort Sill
Lt. Col. John P. Hatch
4th Cav, 4 Cos.
1st Arty, 4 Cos.
2nd Arty, 1 Co.
23 officers, 501 enlisted

Fort Reno
Maj. J.K. Mizner
4th Cav, 2 Cos.
2nd Arty, 1 Co.
3rd Arty, 2 Cos.
16 officers, 312 enlisted

Camp Supply
Capt. P.H. Remington
19th Inf, 2 Cos.
5 officers, 76 enlisted

New Mexico

District of New Mexico, Santa Fe
Col. Edward Hatch
District Staff, 9th Cav HQ.
8 officers, 29 enlisted

Fort Marcy
Capt. Chambers McKibbin
15th Inf, 1 Co.
2 officers, 52 enlisted

Fort Bayard
Maj. A.P. Morrow
9th Cav, 2 Cos.; 15th Inf, 1 Co.
9 officers, 139 enlisted

Fort Craig
Capt. George Shorkley
15th Inf, 1 Co.
3 officers, 56 enlisted

Fort McRae
Capt. Oscar Hagen
9th Cav, 1 Co.
2 officers, 54 enlisted

Fort Selden
Capt. Charles Steelhammer
9th Cav and 15th Inf, 2 Cos.
5 officers, 88 enlisted

Fort Stanton
Capt. George Remington
9th Cav and 15th Inf, 3 Cos.
6 officers, 172 enlisted

Fort Union
Maj. J.F. Wade
9th Cav, 2 Cos.; 15th Inf, 2 Cos.
18 officers, 258 enlisted

Fort Wingate
Maj. N.W Osborne
9th Cav and 15th Inf, HQ, 3 Cos.
13 officer, 255 enlisted

sergeant, commissary sergeant, saddler sergeant, chief trumpeter, and a hospital steward. Additionally, the regiment had a chief musician and a band of about 20 members. The regimental staff had to oversee all the operations of its widely dispersed companies throughout the division. The Army authorized a chaplain to African-American regiments who also served as an instructor to teach reading and writing to soldiers.

Unit composition of the Department of the Missouri in September 1876.

(continues on page 38)

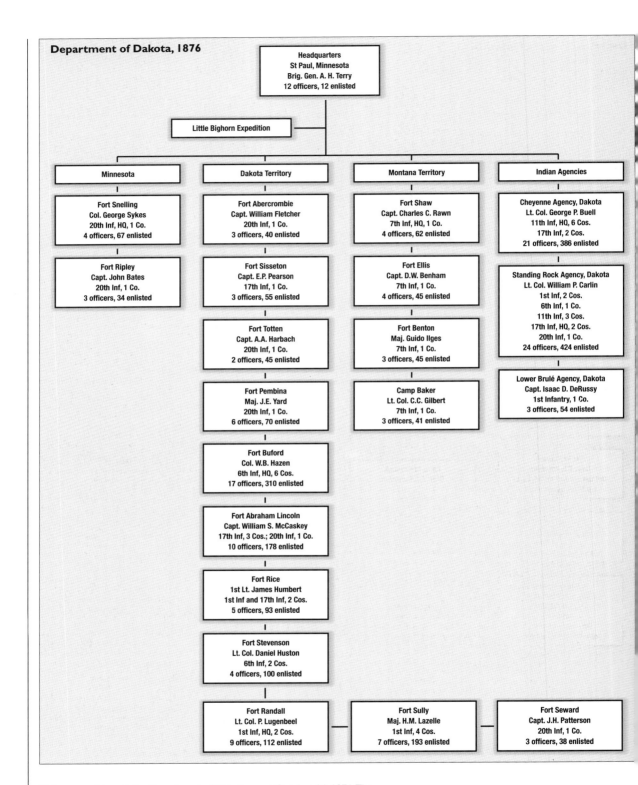

Department of Dakota, 1876

Headquarters
St Paul, Minnesota
Brig. Gen. A. H. Terry
12 officers, 12 enlisted

Little Bighorn Expedition

Minnesota	Dakota Territory	Montana Territory	Indian Agencies

Fort Snelling
Col. George Sykes
20th Inf, HQ, 1 Co.
4 officers, 67 enlisted

Fort Abercrombie
Capt. William Fletcher
20th Inf, 1 Co.
3 officers, 40 enlisted

Fort Shaw
Capt. Charles C. Rawn
7th Inf, HQ, 1 Co.
4 officers, 62 enlisted

Cheyenne Agency, Dakota
Lt. Col. George P. Buell
11th Inf, HQ, 6 Cos.
17th Inf, 2 Cos.
21 officers, 386 enlisted

Fort Ripley
Capt. John Bates
20th Inf, 1 Co.
3 officers, 34 enlisted

Fort Sisseton
Capt. E.P. Pearson
17th Inf, 1 Co.
3 officers, 55 enlisted

Fort Ellis
Capt. D.W. Benham
7th Inf, 1 Co.
4 officers, 45 enlisted

Standing Rock Agency, Dakota
Lt. Col. William P. Carlin
1st Inf, 2 Cos.
6th Inf, 1 Co.
11th Inf, 3 Cos.
17th Inf, HQ, 2 Cos.
20th Inf, 1 Co.
24 officers, 424 enlisted

Fort Totten
Capt. A.A. Harbach
20th Inf, 1 Co.
2 officers, 45 enlisted

Fort Benton
Maj. Guido Ilges
7th Inf, 1 Co.
3 officers, 45 enlisted

Lower Brulé Agency, Dakota
Capt. Isaac D. DeRussy
1st Infantry, 1 Co.
3 officers, 54 enlisted

Fort Pembina
Maj. J.E. Yard
20th Inf, 1 Co.
6 officers, 70 enlisted

Camp Baker
Lt. Col. C.C. Gilbert
7th Inf, 1 Co.
3 officers, 41 enlisted

Fort Buford
Col. W.B. Hazen
6th Inf, HQ, 6 Cos.
17 officers, 310 enlisted

Fort Abraham Lincoln
Capt. William S. McCaskey
17th Inf, 3 Cos.; 20th Inf, 1 Co.
10 officers, 178 enlisted

Fort Rice
1st Lt. James Humbert
1st Inf and 17th Inf, 2 Cos.
5 officers, 93 enlisted

Fort Stevenson
Lt. Col. Daniel Huston
6th Inf, 2 Cos.
4 officers, 100 enlisted

Fort Randall
Lt. Col. P. Lugenbeel
1st Inf, HQ, 2 Cos.
9 officers, 112 enlisted

Fort Sully
Maj. H.M. Lazelle
1st Inf, 4 Cos.
7 officers, 193 enlisted

Fort Seward
Capt. J.H. Patterson
20th Inf, 1 Co.
3 officers, 38 enlisted

Unit composition of the Department of Dakota, as at October 14, 1876. The
department's contribution to the Little Big Horn expedition was led by Brig. Gen.
Alfred H. Terry and was composed of units from the 2nd and 7th Cavalry and 5th,
6th, 7th, 17th, and 22nd Infantry. A total of 41 companies participated from the
department, comprising 104 officers and 1,749 enlisted men.

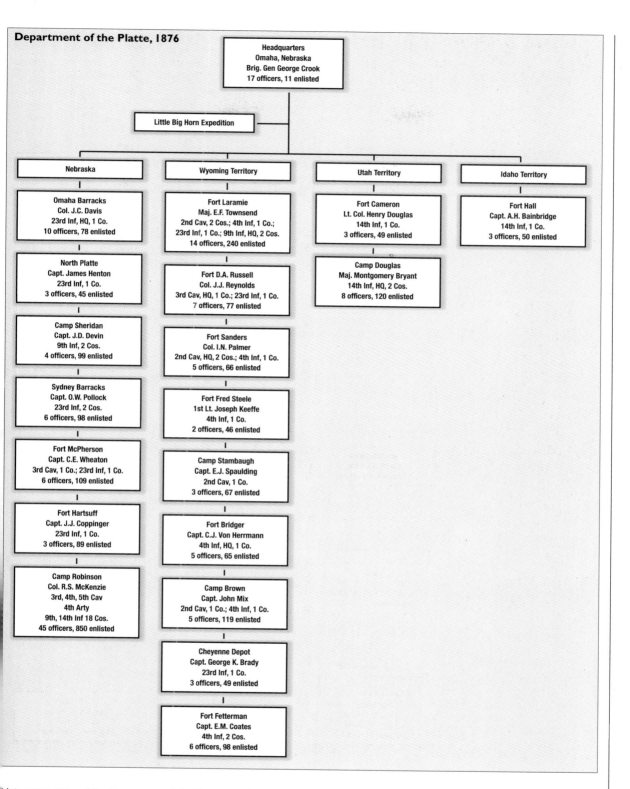

Department of the Platte, 1876

Headquarters
Omaha, Nebraska
Brig. Gen George Crook
17 officers, 11 enlisted

Little Big Horn Expedition

Nebraska

Omaha Barracks
Col. J.C. Davis
23rd Inf, HQ, 1 Co.
10 officers, 78 enlisted

North Platte
Capt. James Henton
23rd Inf, 1 Co.
3 officers, 45 enlisted

Camp Sheridan
Capt. J.D. Devin
9th Inf, 2 Cos.
4 officers, 99 enlisted

Sydney Barracks
Capt. O.W. Pollock
23rd Inf, 2 Cos.
6 officers, 98 enlisted

Fort McPherson
Capt. C.E. Wheaton
3rd Cav, 1 Co.; 23rd Inf, 1 Co.
6 officers, 109 enlisted

Fort Hartsuff
Capt. J.J. Coppinger
23rd Inf, 1 Co.
3 officers, 89 enlisted

Camp Robinson
Col. R.S. McKenzie
3rd, 4th, 5th Cav
4th Arty
9th, 14th Inf 18 Cos.
45 officers, 850 enlisted

Wyoming Territory

Fort Laramie
Maj. E.F. Townsend
2nd Cav, 2 Cos.; 4th Inf, 1 Co.;
23rd Inf, 1 Co.; 9th Inf, HQ, 2 Cos.
14 officers, 240 enlisted

Fort D.A. Russell
Col. J.J. Reynolds
3rd Cav, HQ, 1 Co.; 23rd Inf, 1 Co.
7 officers, 77 enlisted

Fort Sanders
Col. I.N. Palmer
2nd Cav, HQ, 2 Cos.; 4th Inf, 1 Co.
5 officers, 66 enlisted

Fort Fred Steele
1st Lt. Joseph Keeffe
4th Inf, 1 Co.
2 officers, 46 enlisted

Camp Stambaugh
Capt. E.J. Spaulding
2nd Cav, 1 Co.
3 officers, 67 enlisted

Fort Bridger
Capt. C.J. Von Herrmann
4th Inf, HQ, 1 Co.
5 officers, 65 enlisted

Camp Brown
Capt. John Mix
2nd Cav, 1 Co.; 4th Inf, 1 Co.
5 officers, 119 enlisted

Cheyenne Depot
Capt. George K. Brady
23rd Inf, 1 Co.
3 officers, 49 enlisted

Fort Fetterman
Capt. E.M. Coates
4th Inf, 2 Cos.
6 officers, 98 enlisted

Utah Territory

Fort Cameron
Lt. Col. Henry Douglas
14th Inf, 1 Co.
3 officers, 49 enlisted

Camp Douglas
Maj. Montgomery Bryant
14th Inf, HQ, 2 Cos.
8 officers, 120 enlisted

Idaho Territory

Fort Hall
Capt. A.H. Bainbridge
14th Inf, 1 Co.
3 officers, 50 enlisted

Unit composition of the Department of the Platte as at October 14, 1876. The department's contribution to the Little Big Horn expedition was led by Brig. Gen. George Crook and was composed of units from the 2nd, 3rd, and 5th Cavalry and the 4th, 9th, and 14th Infantry. Crook had 35 companies with 84 officers and 1,428 enlisted men.

The artillery and infantry regimental headquarters were staffed as per the cavalry. Colonels commanded these regiments, with lieutenant-colonels second in command. However, unlike the artillery and cavalry, the infantry regiment had only one major compared to three majors in the other branches.

The total authorized strength for regiments varied. Units assigned to areas where hostilities were underway were authorized an increase in personnel. Cavalry regiments typically contained between 888 and 1,249 personnel in 1876. For example, the 7th Cavalry had 1,249 authorized while the 1st Cavalry, headquartered in the San Francisco Bay area (Benecia Barracks) in California, had only 888. The strength of infantry regiments ranged from 341 to 580 men. An artillery regiment contained from 496 to 616 soldiers.

A typical regiment was divided into several companies. For example, a cavalry regiment was authorized to maintain 12 companies, later renamed "troops" in October 1881. The companies were given an alphabetic designation ranging from A to M. By 1891, companies L and M had been eliminated and the regiment reverted to ten companies. The personnel of these disbanded companies was distributed throughout the remainder of the regiment. In infantry and cavalry units, the enlisted men were integrated into the other companies to increase their combat capability, and officers were released for special duties. Each cavalry company typically had fewer than 100 officers and men.

An artillery regiment had slightly fewer soldiers, being organized around 12 companies or batteries. Strength varied, but was usually around 40 men. The infantry regiment had only 10 companies, designated from A to K. In total, the Army maintained 430 companies on about 200 frontier posts.

The regimental system did not include an effective battalion structure in the post-Civil War reorganization. This intermediate organization was all but eliminated in tables of organization, although the companies of an entire regiment were organized into one battalion purely to keep the organizational structure alive due to legal necessity. Several officers complained about this system, but it remained in effect, at least on paper, to the end of the Plains Indian Wars. Army reformers in 1891 continued to disagree about the lack of an effective battalion structure. One proposal was to reorganize infantry regiments into three battalions of four companies apiece.

Although the battalion as a permanent organization was largely ignored, as a temporary measure field commanders pressed this organization into service under field conditions. Regiments on campaign could deploy up to 12 companies at a time, depending on the branch. Similarly, an expedition might consist of several artillery, infantry, or cavalry companies. Commanders would have to orchestrate the support, maneuvering, and actions of companies that varied greatly in size, experience, and capability. Coordination between individual company commanders and their regimental commander would likewise suffer, so temporary battalions were formed during expeditions, or whenever a commander felt better command and control of troops would result.

A field battalion would consist of at least two companies. For example, during the Powder River campaign of February 1876, an unsuccessful campaign against the Sioux that led to the Little Big Horn expedition, two-company battalions were employed. The expedition was formed with elements of the 2nd and 3rd Cavalry and the 4th Infantry. Each cavalry regiment contributed five companies apiece, with two companies from the infantry regiment. In all six battalions were formed.

During the Little Big Horn expedition, George Custer commanded all of 7th Cavalry up to the point of discovery of their objective, the Sioux encampments. He then divided his 12 companies into battalions. Custer retained five companies while forming two other combat battalions of three companies each. The battalion commanders would lead their respective elements on the field to search for and attack any band of warriors they encountered. Custer issued orders to each battalion commander, who was the senior company commander, and allowed each to conduct operations using his own initiative. Custer also formed a separate support column with a pack train with a company for protection.

In the late-1880s, cavalry battalions were designated "squadrons." Commanders resurrected the battalion in the field, although eliminated on paper, to meet a particular situation and then just as quickly disbanded them after the Army resolved the condition.

Regiments were normally assigned to particular geographic divisions. Usually, subordinate units were kept within their parent division or department. There were exceptions. Some companies were sent temporarily to support other departments or permanently assigned there. For example, the 7th Cavalry had three of its companies assigned outside of the Department of Dakota to the Department of the Gulf. Other regiments had companies dispersed between different divisions and departments. The 3rd Artillery Regiment had companies in New York, South Carolina, Kansas, and the Indian Territories (Oklahoma). A regiment was rarely kept together on one post. Thus regiments became administrative units in name only. Frequently, a regiment's companies might be separated for years and not fight together unless on an extended campaign. Where once regiments were the focal point of military activities, companies became the key operational units.

Consequently many posts contained companies that came from different regiments. For example, in 1876 Fort Dodge, Kansas (under the Department of the Missouri) had two companies, one from the 2nd Artillery Regiment and the other from the 19th Infantry Regiment. These posts were frequently populated with fewer than 100 soldiers, sometimes with an artillery piece or a Gatling gun. Some units had nothing more in common than a shared regimental designation.

The company

The company lay at the heart of the frontier army, providing a financial, administrative, and operational focal point. Typical encounters with Indians, either on patrol or in combat, were at the company level. Soldiers would serve out entire enlistments and careers in a single company: they lived, ate, slept, fought, and died within their unit. Veteran officers and non-commissioned officers provided the stability and experience to shape the company into an effective fighting machine.

An infantry company was authorized two platoons and support in 1876.

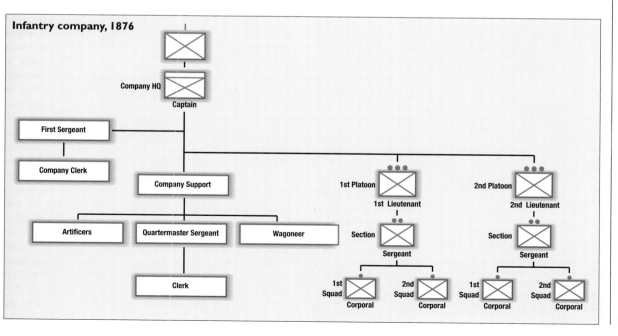

Infantry company, 1876

Company HQ — Captain

First Sergeant

Company Clerk

Company Support

Artificers — Quartermaster Sergeant — Wagoneer

Clerk

1st Platoon — 1st Lieutenant
Section — Sergeant
1st Squad — Corporal
2nd Squad — Corporal

2nd Platoon — 2nd Lieutenant
Section — Sergeant
1st Squad — Corporal
2nd Squad — Corporal

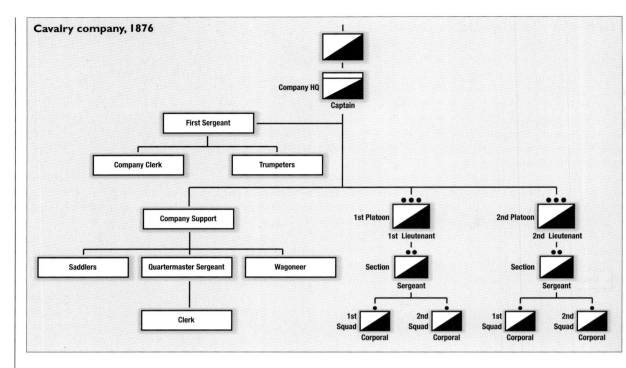

Cavalry company, 1876

Company HQ — Captain

First Sergeant

Company Clerk — Trumpeters

Company Support

Saddlers — Quartermaster Sergeant — Wagoneer

Clerk

1st Platoon — 1st Lieutenant
Section — Sergeant
1st Squad — Corporal
2nd Squad — Corporal

2nd Platoon — 2nd Lieutenant
Section — Sergeant
1st Squad — Corporal
2nd Squad — Corporal

Typical cavalry company structure, c. 1876.

There were definite advantages to this stable relationship. Officers and enlisted men knew the capabilities of each member of the company, after years of close affiliation and combat testing. Transfers of officers or enlisted men out of the company were highly unusual. Additionally, companies were not moved unless the post was closed or the entire regiment transferred out of the department. The relationship between officers and men was thus close, and each soldier had to rely on his fellow company members. Soldiers knew their officers' and non-commissioned officers' leadership style, strengths, weaknesses, and general tactics, as well as the local environment and threats their company had to face everyday. Unit cohesion became necessary to survive both the danger and the boredom of frontier life, in the face of inevitable tension or friction between company members. The esprit de corps that was lost in the reorganization of regiments was replaced on a smaller scale within the company.

The company had an organization and staffing similar to that of the regimental headquarters. In 1876, a cavalry company commander was usually a

Army posts were home to self-contained communities, and did not normally feature extensive fortifications. This 1880 photograph shows Fort Missoula, Montana. (RG315 Daughters of the US Army .97)

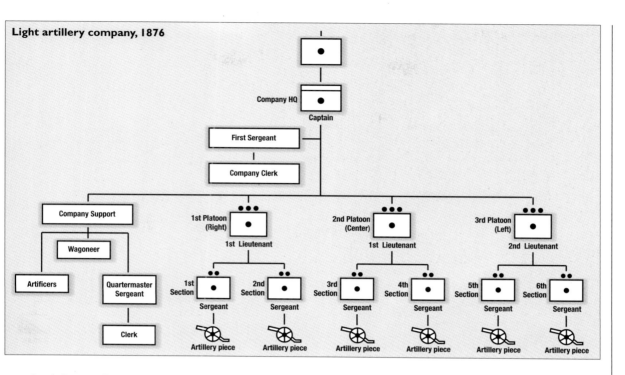

Light artillery company, 1876

Company HQ — Captain

First Sergeant

Company Clerk

Company Support

Wagoneer

Artificers

Quartermaster Sergeant

Clerk

1st Platoon (Right) — 1st Lieutenant

2nd Platoon (Center) — 1st Lieutenant

3rd Platoon (Left) — 2nd Lieutenant

1st Section — Sergeant — Artillery piece

2nd Section — Sergeant — Artillery piece

3rd Section — Sergeant — Artillery piece

4th Section — Sergeant — Artillery piece

5th Section — Sergeant — Artillery piece

6th Section — Sergeant — Artillery piece

captain. A first- and second-lieutenant assisted him. The company first-sergeant, a quartermaster sergeant, and a commissary sergeant further aided these officers. Later, a medical officer was added to support post hospitals. Contract surgeons were also hired in lieu of military doctors. The company also contained five sergeants, four corporals, two trumpeters, a wagoneer, two farriers and blacksmiths, and a saddler.

The infantry company's organization was similar, though it did not require a trumpeter, saddler, or the farriers and blacksmiths. It had two specialists to support operations, such as a soldier to repair equipment or clothing. Most infantry companies were normally assigned only 40 privates. The two African-American infantry regiments had even fewer authorized personnel, but the small numbers did not hinder recruitment or retention. These African-American regiments actually retained more men than authorized, as did some standard regiments.

The artillery company was authorized a captain as its commander. Congress did authorize an additional first-lieutenant to be assigned to the company to help with logistics or command an extra platoon of cannon. The Army designated

In 1876, light artillery companies contained six artillery pieces.

Once established, Plains posts took on the feel and look of Eastern installations. These officer quarters at Fort Leavenworth, Kansas, were photographed in 1883, yet seem elegant even today. (RG126 W.C. Brown .151)

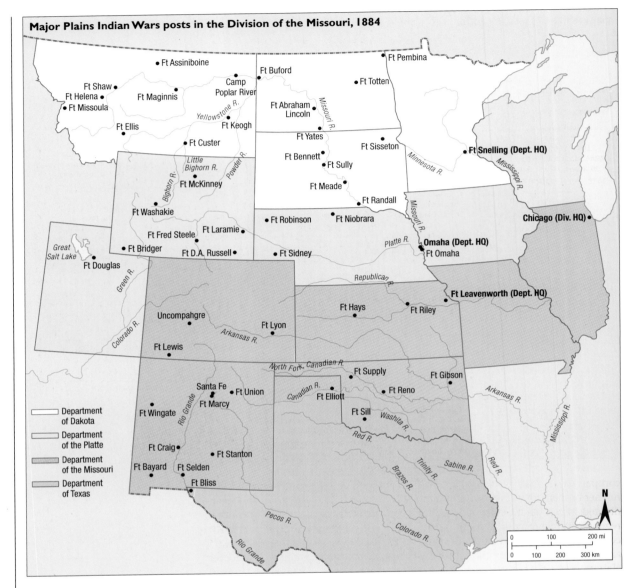

Major Plains Indian Wars posts in the Division of the Missouri, 1884

Ft Assiniboine

Ft Shaw
Ft Helena
Ft Missoula
Ft Maginnis

Camp
Poplar River

Ft Buford

Ft Pembina

Ft Totten

Ft Ellis

Yellowstone R.

Ft Keogh

Ft Abraham
Lincoln

Missouri R.

Ft Snelling (Dept. HQ)

Ft Custer

Little
Bighorn R.

Ft Yates

Ft Sisseton

Minnesota R.

Mississippi R.

Ft Bennett

Bighorn R.

Ft McKinney

Powder R.

Ft Sully

Ft Washakie

Ft Meade

Ft Randall

Missouri R.

Chicago (Div. HQ)

Ft Fred Steele

Ft Laramie

Ft Robinson

Ft Niobrara

Great
Salt Lake

Ft Bridger

Ft D.A. Russell

Platte R.

Omaha (Dept. HQ)
Ft Omaha

Ft Douglas

Ft Sidney

Green R.

Republican R.

Ft Leavenworth (Dept. HQ)

Uncompahgre

Ft Hays

Ft Riley

Ft Lyon

Colorado R.

Arkansas R.

Ft Lewis

North Fork, Canadian R.

Ft Supply

Ft Gibson

Arkansas R.

Santa Fe

Ft Union

Canadian R.

Ft Reno

Mississippi R.

Ft Wingate

Ft Marcy

Ft Elliott

Ft Sill

Washita R.

Rio Grande

Ft Craig

Ft Stanton

Red R.

Ft Bayard

Ft Selden

Brazos R.

Trinity R.

Sabine R.

Red R.

Ft Bliss

Pecos R.

Colorado R.

Rio Grande

Department
of Dakota

Department
of the Platte

Department
of the Missouri

Department
of Texas

N

0   100   200 mi
0   100   200   300 km

units as either a company or a battery. Artillery batteries normally had more soldiers than the companies. These batteries were assigned to important fortifications that protected seaports on the East, Gulf, and West coasts. For example, Battery A of the 2nd Artillery Regiment was located at Fort McHenry, Maryland. The battery's mission, with its 70 personnel, was to protect Baltimore's vital harbor. By the 1880s, artillery companies were often referred to as batteries whether they were defending the seacoast or not. The light artillery companies comprised horse, field, and mountain units, and differed from infantry units by having four artificers and between 20 and 40 privates. Artillery artificers were specialists that supported artillery operations, repairing or providing technical support for the cannons

There were subordinate units for cavalry, infantry, and artillery companies, troops, and batteries. Drill regulations suggested an infantry company be organized into two equal-sized platoons, with a lieutenant in command of each: the company's first-lieutenant commanded the first platoon, while the junior lieutenant, normally a second-lieutenant, guided the second platoon. If the

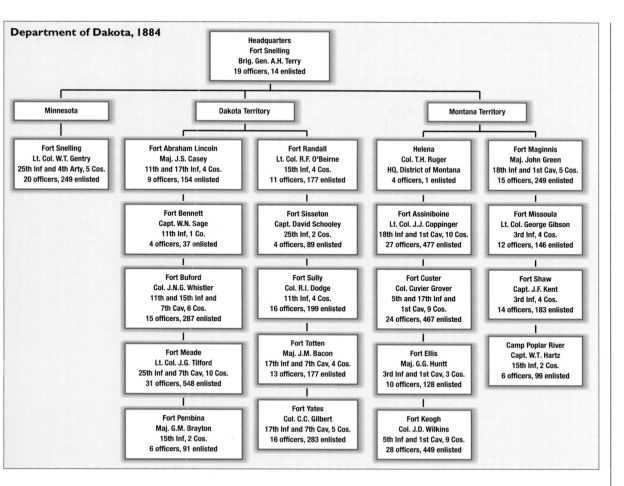

Department of Dakota, 1884

Headquarters
Fort Snelling
Brig. Gen. A.H. Terry
19 officers, 14 enlisted

Minnesota

Dakota Territory

Montana Territory

Fort Snelling
Lt. Col. W.T. Gentry
25th Inf and 4th Arty, 5 Cos.
20 officers, 249 enlisted

Fort Abraham Lincoln
Maj. J.S. Casey
11th and 17th Inf, 4 Cos.
9 officers, 154 enlisted

Fort Randall
Lt. Col. R.F. O'Beirne
15th Inf, 4 Cos.
11 officers, 177 enlisted

Helena
Col. T.H. Ruger
HQ, District of Montana
4 officers, 1 enlisted

Fort Maginnis
Maj. John Green
18th Inf and 1st Cav, 5 Cos.
15 officers, 249 enlisted

Fort Bennett
Capt. W.N. Sage
11th Inf, 1 Co.
4 officers, 37 enlisted

Fort Sisseton
Capt. David Schooley
25th Inf, 2 Cos.
4 officers, 89 enlisted

Fort Assiniboine
Lt. Col. J.J. Coppinger
18th Inf and 1st Cav, 10 Cos.
27 officers, 477 enlisted

Fort Missoula
Lt. Col. George Gibson
3rd Inf, 4 Cos.
12 officers, 146 enlisted

Fort Buford
Col. J.N.G. Whistler
11th and 15th Inf and
7th Cav, 6 Cos.
15 officers, 287 enlisted

Fort Sully
Col. R.I. Dodge
11th Inf, 4 Cos.
16 officers, 199 enlisted

Fort Custer
Col. Cuvier Grover
5th and 17th Inf and
1st Cav, 9 Cos.
24 officers, 467 enlisted

Fort Shaw
Capt. J.F. Kent
3rd Inf, 4 Cos.
14 officers, 183 enlisted

Fort Meade
Lt. Col. J.G. Tilford
25th Inf and 7th Cav, 10 Cos.
31 officers, 548 enlisted

Fort Totten
Maj. J.M. Bacon
17th Inf and 7th Cav, 4 Cos.
13 officers, 177 enlisted

Fort Ellis
Maj. G.G. Huntt
3rd Inf and 1st Cav, 3 Cos.
10 officers, 128 enlisted

Camp Poplar River
Capt. W.T. Hartz
15th Inf, 2 Cos.
6 officers, 99 enlisted

Fort Pembina
Maj. G.M. Brayton
15th Inf, 2 Cos.
6 officers, 91 enlisted

Fort Yates
Col. C.C. Gilbert
17th Inf and 7th Cav, 5 Cos.
16 officers, 283 enlisted

Fort Keogh
Col. J.D. Wilkins
5th Inf and 1st Cav, 9 Cos.
28 officers, 449 enlisted

company was relatively small, then the platoons were omitted. Platoons were further broken down into two sections led by sergeants. The sections were further divided into at least two squads led by a non-commissioned officer. Period drill regulations recommended a squad have a non-commissioned officer, normally a corporal, and seven privates. The *Regulations of the United States Army* for 1861, and its next revision in 1881, specified four squads per company, but did not elaborate on other organizational elements. Emory Upton, a key Army reformer of the period that we shall return to later, suggested the company's men should be organized into groups of four since this was the optimal number of personnel a leader could directly supervise, with squads thus becoming two groups of four. These subordinate company units were given a sequential numeric designation. For example, the two platoons were designated either the first or second platoon.

Cavalry units were similarly organized into platoons, sections, and squads. Dismounted cavalry would act like infantry in combat, with the exception that one cavalryman from the section of four would have to watch or picket the horses—which obviously reduced available firepower by a quarter.

The artillery company was organized around the field pieces. An artillery company or battery consisted of two or three platoons. If the artillery company consisted of Gatling guns, then the company might have four or five platoons. A lieutenant commanded each platoon. Individual platoons had two sections, each led by a sergeant. The typical artillery company consisted of six artillery pieces. The artillery section centered on a single artillery piece and included, if appropriate, the caisson, six horses, equipment, and personnel. These sections had a cannoneer or gunner, driver, horse holders, and others. In addition, the

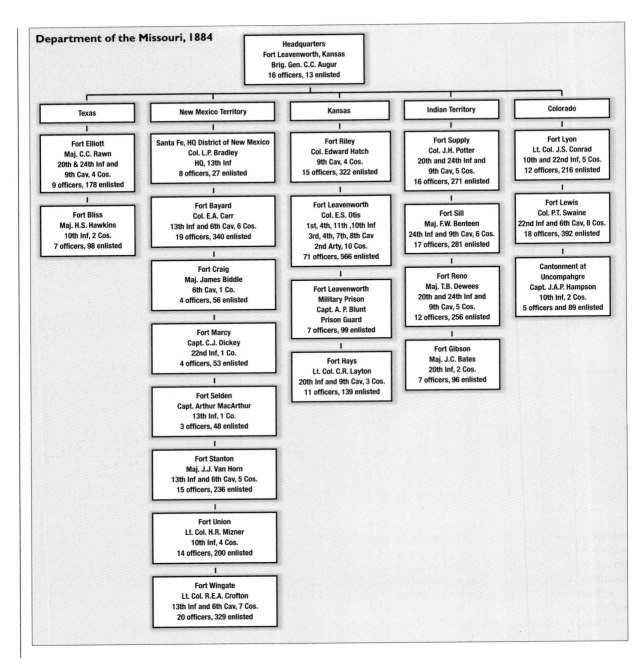

Department of the Missouri, 1884

Headquarters
Fort Leavenworth, Kansas
Brig. Gen. C.C. Augur
16 officers, 13 enlisted

Texas

Fort Elliott
Maj. C.C. Rawn
20th & 24th Inf and
9th Cav, 4 Cos.
9 officers, 178 enlisted

Fort Bliss
Maj. H.S. Hawkins
10th Inf, 2 Cos.
7 officers, 98 enlisted

New Mexico Territory

Santa Fe, HQ District of New Mexico
Col. L.P. Bradley
HQ, 13th Inf
8 officers, 27 enlisted

Fort Bayard
Col. E.A. Carr
13th Inf and 6th Cav, 6 Cos.
19 officers, 340 enlisted

Fort Craig
Maj. James Biddle
6th Cav, 1 Co.
4 officers, 56 enlisted

Fort Marcy
Capt. C.J. Dickey
22nd Inf, 1 Co.
4 officers, 53 enlisted

Fort Selden
Capt. Arthur MacArthur
13th Inf, 1 Co.
3 officers, 48 enlisted

Fort Stanton
Maj. J.J. Van Horn
13th Inf and 6th Cav, 5 Cos.
15 officers, 236 enlisted

Fort Union
Lt. Col. H.R. Mizner
10th Inf, 4 Cos.
14 officers, 200 enlisted

Fort Wingate
Lt. Col. R.E.A. Crofton
13th Inf and 6th Cav, 7 Cos.
20 officers, 329 enlisted

Kansas

Fort Riley
Col. Edward Hatch
9th Cav, 4 Cos.
15 officers, 322 enlisted

Fort Leavenworth
Col. E.S. Otis
1st, 4th, 11th ,10th Inf
3rd, 4th, 7th, 8th Cav
2nd Arty, 10 Cos.
71 officers, 566 enlisted

Fort Leavenworth Military Prison
Capt. A. P. Blunt
Prison Guard
7 officers, 99 enlisted

Fort Hays
Lt. Col. C.R. Layton
20th Inf and 9th Cav, 3 Cos.
11 officers, 139 enlisted

Indian Territory

Fort Supply
Col. J.H. Potter
20th and 24th Inf and
9th Cav, 5 Cos.
16 officers, 271 enlisted

Fort Sill
Maj. F.W. Benteen
24th Inf and 9th Cav, 6 Cos.
17 officers, 281 enlisted

Fort Reno
Maj. T.B. Dewees
20th and 24th Inf and
9th Cav, 5 Cos.
12 officers, 256 enlisted

Fort Gibson
Maj. J.C. Bates
20th Inf, 2 Cos.
7 officers, 96 enlisted

Colorado

Fort Lyon
Lt. Col. J.S. Conrad
10th and 22nd Inf, 5 Cos.
12 officers, 216 enlisted

Fort Lewis
Col. P.T. Swaine
22nd Inf and 6th Cav, 8 Cos.
18 officers, 392 enlisted

Cantonment at Uncompahgre
Capt. J.A.P. Hampson
10th Inf, 2 Cos.
5 officers and 89 enlisted

Army assigned two corporals and five privates to the artillery section. If the section operated a heavy artillery piece, such as at a seacoast fortification, then two additional privates were assigned. Unlike an infantry or cavalry company, artillery companies could have up to three platoons. Since artillery deployed in a line, the 1st platoon was located on the right, the 2nd served on the center, and the 3rd on the left. The companies also had a wagoneer for transport.

Although Congress had set limits on total enlistments for the Army, the actual strength of units varied greatly from the authorized numbers, with the post-Civil War companies normally short of personnel. The 1867 *Report of the Secretary of War* indicated that the number of recruits required to fill authorized regiments and companies was 13,134. If the Army excluded West Point cadets, and personnel either at depots or en route to their post assignments, the

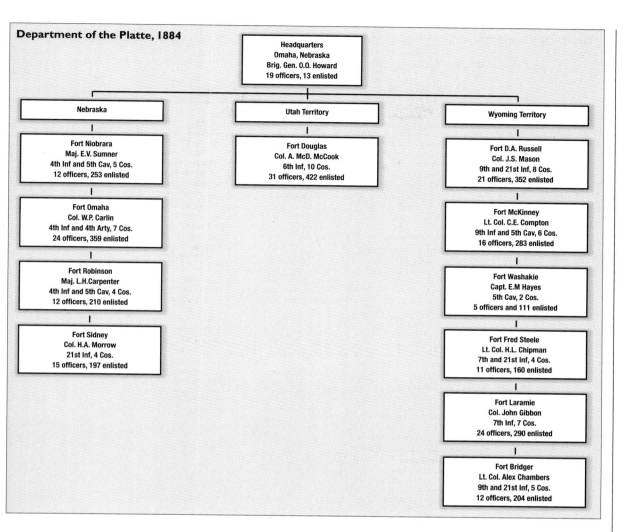

Department of the Platte, 1884

Headquarters
Omaha, Nebraska
Brig. Gen. O.O. Howard
19 officers, 13 enlisted

Nebraska

Fort Niobrara
Maj. E.V. Sumner
4th Inf and 5th Cav, 5 Cos.
12 officers, 253 enlisted

Fort Omaha
Col. W.P. Carlin
4th Inf and 4th Arty, 7 Cos.
24 officers, 359 enlisted

Fort Robinson
Maj. L.H.Carpenter
4th Inf and 5th Cav, 4 Cos.
12 officers, 210 enlisted

Fort Sidney
Col. H.A. Morrow
21st Inf, 4 Cos.
15 officers, 197 enlisted

Utah Territory

Fort Douglas
Col. A. McD. McCook
6th Inf, 10 Cos.
31 officers, 422 enlisted

Wyoming Territory

Fort D.A. Russell
Col. J.S. Mason
9th and 21st Inf, 8 Cos.
21 officers, 352 enlisted

Fort McKinney
Lt. Col. C.E. Compton
9th Inf and 5th Cav, 6 Cos.
16 officers, 283 enlisted

Fort Washakie
Capt. E.M Hayes
5th Cav, 2 Cos.
5 officers and 111 enlisted

Fort Fred Steele
Lt. Col. H.L. Chipman
7th and 21st Inf, 4 Cos.
11 officers, 160 enlisted

Fort Laramie
Col. John Gibbon
7th Inf, 7 Cos.
24 officers, 290 enlisted

Fort Bridger
Lt. Col. Alex Chambers
9th and 21st Inf, 5 Cos.
12 officers, 204 enlisted

number dropped to 6,800. In 1868, Congress allocated funding to allow up to 52,963 soldiers to fill the ranks, but by 1884 reduced funding had slashed personnel to 27,647. Despite this drastic reduction, the Army was still short of its authorized strength by over 1,300 recruits.

Fortunately, the commissioned ranks were consistently kept at full authorization. In 1884, there were 2,147 commissioned officers authorized, the same number as actual strength. The shortages were all in the enlisted ranks, particularly in the infantry. Although the overall shortages may seem small, as a result company strength was less than optimal.

Desertion

Duty on the frontier was harsh, isolated, and dangerous. Low pay and miserable living conditions made Army life hard to accept for many new recruits and veterans. Desertions were relatively high during the Plains Indian Wars, with some even willing to risk the death penalty for leaving while their units were under fire. Approximately one third of all enlistments from 1867 to 1891 ended in some form of desertion: of the 255,712 enlisted men in the period, 88,475 soldiers deserted. Rates overall averaged between 25 and 40 percent per year during the Plains Indian Wars, whereas during the Civil War (where soldiers faced a greater chance of being killed or maimed) the desertion rate averaged only 14.8 percent. Desertion resulted in the immediate loss of a trained combat

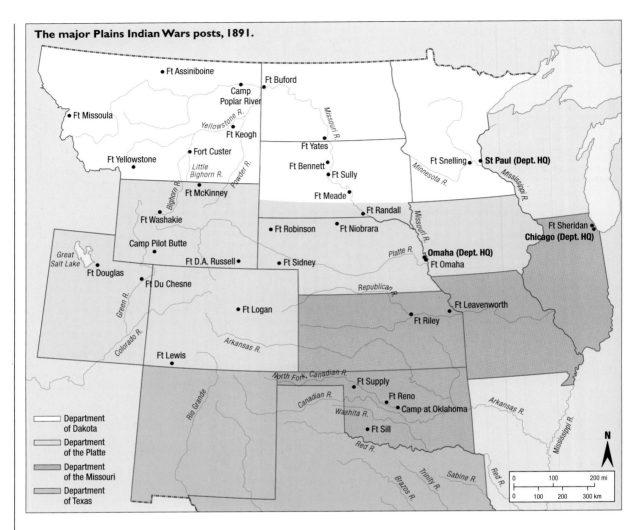

The major Plains Indian Wars posts, 1891.

- Ft Assiniboine
- Ft Buford
- Camp Poplar River
- Ft Missoula
- Yellowstone R.
- Ft Keogh
- Ft Yellowstone
- Fort Custer
- Little Bighorn R.
- Powder R.
- Missouri R.
- Ft Yates
- Ft Bennett
- Ft Sully
- Ft Snelling
- St Paul (Dept. HQ)
- Minnesota R.
- Mississippi R.
- Ft McKinney
- Bighorn R.
- Ft Meade
- Ft Washakie
- Camp Pilot Butte
- Ft Randall
- Ft Robinson
- Ft Niobrara
- Ft Sheridan
- Chicago (Dept. HQ)
- Great Salt Lake
- Ft D.A. Russell
- Ft Sidney
- Platte R.
- Omaha (Dept. HQ)
- Ft Omaha
- Ft Douglas
- Ft Du Chesne
- Green R.
- Republican R.
- Colorado R.
- Ft Logan
- Ft Leavenworth
- Ft Riley
- Arkansas R.
- Ft Lewis
- Rio Grande
- North Fork, Canadian R.
- Ft Supply
- Canadian R.
- Ft Reno
- Camp at Oklahoma
- Arkansas R.
- Washita R.
- Ft Sill
- Red R.
- Mississippi R.
- Sabine R.
- Brazos R.
- Trinity R.
- Red R.

Department of Dakota
Department of the Platte
Department of the Missouri
Department of Texas

0   100   200 mi
0   100   200   300 km

N

By 1891, the Division of the Missouri had been abolished, but the departments remained. Although forts Brady, Makinac and Wayne were part of the Department of the Missouri, they did not play a significant role in the Plains Indian Wars since they were located in Michigan, far to the east of any operations.

soldier who would need to be replaced. Additionally, the missing weapons, uniforms, and horse in the case of a cavalry trooper, added to the damage and financial effect. Desertion also lowered the discipline, morale, and combat efficiency of the remaining soldiers.

Brig. Gen. John Pope, commanding the Department of the Missouri, believed many of the reasons lay in boredom. Pope wrote to the Secretary of War from his headquarters at Fort Leavenworth, Kansas on September 25, 1872 that the average soldier needed more "amusement, mental or physical, than is now possible for him to have." Pope also noted the inadequate pay in comparison to other opportunities for the men to make a better living, like railroad construction or operations positions. Soldiers, in Pope's opinion, had too much idle time after duty to drink, complain, or get into trouble. Providing post-libraries, reading rooms, education, or other diversions might better occupy the attention of the men. The poor living conditions were also thought to provoke soldiers into committing misdemeanors, resulting in fines or confinement as punishment. If a soldier was confined or incapable of performing duties because of this, the other members of the company were forced to perform his duties, which further contributed to discontent.

Maj. Gen. Oliver O. Howard, the Commanding General of the Department of the East, commented in an 1891 report to Schofield that desertions merely reflected the poor quality of the recruits entering service, who appeared more

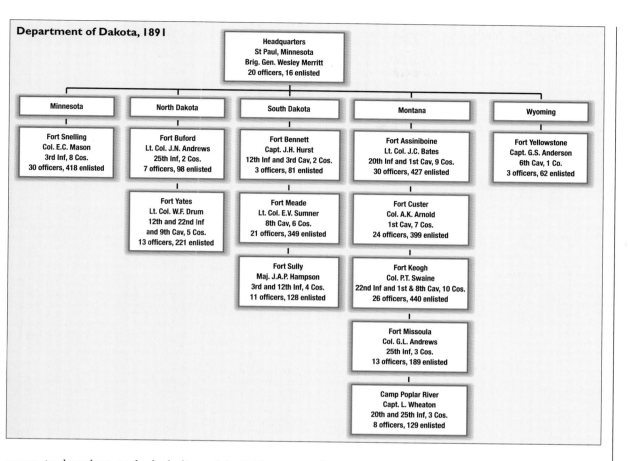

Department of Dakota, 1891

Headquarters
St Paul, Minnesota
Brig. Gen. Wesley Merritt
20 officers, 16 enlisted

Minnesota

North Dakota

South Dakota

Montana

Wyoming

Fort Snelling
Col. E.C. Mason
3rd Inf, 8 Cos.
30 officers, 418 enlisted

Fort Buford
Lt. Col. J.N. Andrews
25th Inf, 2 Cos.
7 officers, 98 enlisted

Fort Bennett
Capt. J.H. Hurst
12th Inf and 3rd Cav, 2 Cos.
3 officers, 81 enlisted

Fort Assiniboine
Lt. Col. J.C. Bates
20th Inf and 1st Cav, 9 Cos.
30 officers, 427 enlisted

Fort Yellowstone
Capt. G.S. Anderson
6th Cav, 1 Co.
3 officers, 62 enlisted

Fort Yates
Lt. Col. W.F. Drum
12th and 22nd Inf
and 9th Cav, 5 Cos.
13 officers, 221 enlisted

Fort Meade
Lt. Col. E.V. Sumner
8th Cav, 6 Cos.
21 officers, 349 enlisted

Fort Custer
Col. A.K. Arnold
1st Cav, 7 Cos.
24 officers, 399 enlisted

Fort Sully
Maj. J.A.P. Hampson
3rd and 12th Inf, 4 Cos.
11 officers, 128 enlisted

Fort Keogh
Col. P.T. Swaine
22nd Inf and 1st & 8th Cav, 10 Cos.
26 officers, 440 enlisted

Fort Missoula
Col. G.L. Andrews
25th Inf, 3 Cos.
13 officers, 189 enlisted

Camp Poplar River
Capt. L. Wheaton
20th and 25th Inf, 3 Cos.
8 officers, 129 enlisted

prone to boredom and alcoholism. Schofield attempted to improve the situation by allowing soldiers to purchase their discharge, improving food rations, and overhauling the military justice system.

The chances of a deserter being caught and tried for the offense were slim. In 1867, the Army reported 13,608 desertions, but only 2,998 of those who did so were apprehended or surrendered to the authorities. Some did not even face punishment, being restored to duty without trial. The brunt of the desertions fell upon units that were physically isolated and on campaign, and cavalry units witnessed most of them. E.D. Townsend, Assistant Adjutant General for the War Department, reported that the 2nd, 7th, and 8th cavalry regiments had over 450 desertions each in 1868—a rate of 50 percent or more. One exception to high desertion rates was the 25th Infantry regiment, an African-American regiment serving in the Dakotas and Montana: it had one of the lowest desertion rates in the Army.

Desertion, death, normal discharges, illness, and deployments weakened the company's ability to conduct operations and maintain its post. Such losses challenged company commanders, and Congress's 1870 reduction in military pay did not improve the company's ability to retain seasoned veterans or new recruits. Privates had earned $16 per month after the Civil War: Congress cut this to $13, with other ranks facing similar reductions in pay and, subsequently, morale. The unpopular nature of "peacetime" military service, without a prominent national threat, also created problems for Army recruiters, with the standards lowered as a result. Many recruits came from the growing foreign-born, urban population. These men were usually illiterate, poor, and had few skills as well as often questionable backgrounds. These men filled most of the lower enlisted ranks from 1870 onwards.

The frontier post

Frontier posts or forts were key bastions of American military power throughout the West, and played a vital part in the war. Some of the permanent fortifications built still serve today. Other posts, long forgotten, were temporary facilities built of adobe or rough-hewn lumber. The posts were self-contained encampments from which operations could be launched. If the post was located near an Indian reservation, then Army units could act as a constabulary force to quell uprisings or aid Bureau of Indian Affairs officials. The posts also provided security to cities, settlers, emigrant wagon trains, ranchers, miners, and the railroads. The temporary and permanent post organization also created a grid of forward supply depots to support future operations. The one weakness of the United States Army was its reliance on extensive logical support. Posts could provide some immediate supply help and reduce the length of the supply line on the frontier. These posts were also ready to act as the eyes and ears of the frontier military. Patrols and field reports provided vital information for their departments and the Division of the Missouri to plan for campaigns and other actions.

The Division of the Missouri contained many of the service's active posts during the period, and it was within the departments of the Missouri, Platte, and Dakota that the majority of operations against the Plains Indians were conducted. The early campaigns in 1868 against the Southern Plains Indian tribes after the Civil War involved 26 posts: the departments of Dakota and Platte had only 15 and 11 posts respectively in the period. As the Southern campaigns died down and the Northern Plains Indian campaigns took off, the focus shifted to the departments of Dakota and the Platte. By 1876, the Army had gradually reduced active posts to 20 in the Department of the Missouri while boosting those in Dakota to 21 and in the Platte to 19. As the Plains Indian Wars petered out and budget cuts took effect, the number of posts gradually shrank. The Army had only 10 active posts in the entire Department of the Missouri and 13 in the Platte in 1886. The Dakotas still witnessed Sioux tribal activity and its forces manned 19 posts. The Army had started to consolidate posts by 1891. The Department of Dakota cut its active posts to 12, the Missouri controlled 10 forts and camps, and the Platte maintained its 13 military encampments.

Fort Leavenworth's large troop population and status as departmental headquarters allowed many permanent facilities to be established. As the frontline shifted westwards, its artillery pieces became more ceremonial than operational. (RG24 Guy V. Henry .8)

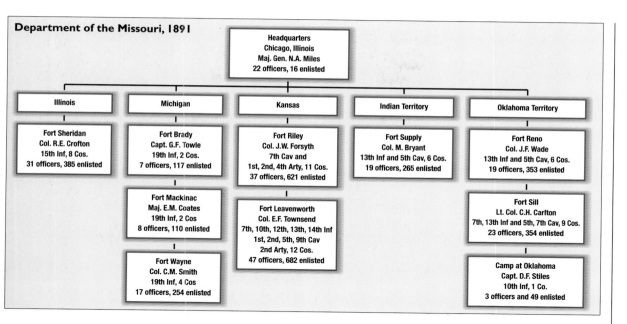

Department of the Missouri, 1891

Headquarters
Chicago, Illinois
Maj. Gen. N.A. Miles
22 officers, 16 enlisted

Illinois

Fort Sheridan
Col. R.E. Crofton
15th Inf, 8 Cos.
31 officers, 385 enlisted

Michigan

Fort Brady
Capt. G.F. Towle
19th Inf, 2 Cos.
7 officers, 117 enlisted

Fort Mackinac
Maj. E.M. Coates
19th Inf, 2 Cos
8 officers, 110 enlisted

Fort Wayne
Col. C.M. Smith
19th Inf, 4 Cos.
17 officers, 254 enlisted

Kansas

Fort Riley
Col. J.W. Forsyth
7th Cav and
1st, 2nd, 4th Arty, 11 Cos.
37 officers, 621 enlisted

Fort Leavenworth
Col. E.F. Townsend
7th, 10th, 12th, 13th, 14th Inf
1st, 2nd, 5th, 9th Cav
2nd Arty, 12 Cos.
47 officers, 682 enlisted

Indian Territory

Fort Supply
Col. M. Bryant
13th Inf and 5th Cav, 6 Cos.
19 officers, 265 enlisted

Oklahoma Territory

Fort Reno
Col. J.F. Wade
13th Inf and 5th Cav, 6 Cos.
19 officers, 353 enlisted

Fort Sill
Lt. Col. C.H. Carlton
7th, 13th Inf and 5th, 7th Cav, 9 Cos.
23 officers, 354 enlisted

Camp at Oklahoma
Capt. D.F. Stiles
10th Inf, 1 Co.
3 officers and 49 enlisted

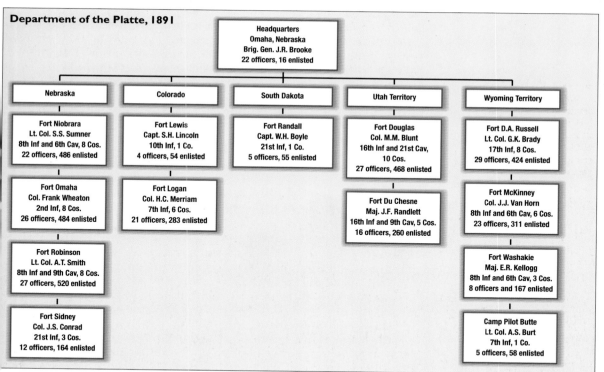

Department of the Platte, 1891

Headquarters
Omaha, Nebraska
Brig. Gen. J.R. Brooke
22 officers, 16 enlisted

Nebraska

Fort Niobrara
Lt. Col. S.S. Sumner
8th Inf and 6th Cav, 8 Cos.
22 officers, 486 enlisted

Fort Omaha
Col. Frank Wheaton
2nd Inf, 8 Cos.
26 officers, 484 enlisted

Fort Robinson
Lt. Col. A.T. Smith
8th Inf and 9th Cav, 8 Cos.
27 officers, 520 enlisted

Fort Sidney
Col. J.S. Conrad
21st Inf, 3 Cos.
12 officers, 164 enlisted

Colorado

Fort Lewis
Capt. S.H. Lincoln
10th Inf, 1 Co.
4 officers, 54 enlisted

Fort Logan
Col. H.C. Merriam
7th Inf, 6 Cos.
21 officers, 283 enlisted

South Dakota

Fort Randall
Capt. W.H. Boyle
21st Inf, 1 Co.
5 officers, 55 enlisted

Utah Territory

Fort Douglas
Col. M.M. Blunt
16th Inf and 21st Cav,
10 Cos.
27 officers, 468 enlisted

Fort Du Chesne
Maj. J.F. Randlett
16th Inf and 9th Cav, 5 Cos.
16 officers, 260 enlisted

Wyoming Territory

Fort D.A. Russell
Lt. Col. G.K. Brady
17th Inf, 8 Cos.
29 officers, 424 enlisted

Fort McKinney
Col. J.J. Van Horn
8th Inf and 6th Cav, 6 Cos.
23 officers, 311 enlisted

Fort Washakie
Maj. E.R. Kellogg
8th Inf and 6th Cav, 3 Cos.
8 officers and 167 enlisted

Camp Pilot Butte
Lt. Col. A.S. Burt
7th Inf, 1 Co.
5 officers, 58 enlisted

At the end of the Plains Indian Wars, the Army primarily needed permanent fortifications on Indian reservations and at other strategic points crucial to the security of the West. In 1884, Schofield, as commander of the Division of the Missouri, indicated that the Army could eliminate many useless posts. On October 14, 1884, in his annual report to the Secretary of War, he wrote: "The tide of civilization has crossed the continent, the Indians have been located on reservations, near which considerable bodies of troops must be stationed to preserve or suppress any outbreak." The grid of outposts created in the early

Some post facilities in the frontier were primitive. The officer quarters shown here were photographed in 1870 at Fort Sill. (RG95 Fort Sill Collection Box 8)

1860s and 1870s was no longer needed to monitor Indian movements. They would only waste manpower and dilute the Army's ability to react to any future Indian uprising.

The true frontier posts were at the edge of hostile territory or near Indian reservations, far from any cities or towns, and were normally far from established lines of supply. Sites that allowed for water, wood, and food were selected. Labor parties of soldiers would gather water, firewood, or timber for construction year round. Although the War Department was responsible for the provision of adequate rations to those outposts, inevitable delays because of weather, lack of transport, bureaucracy, and hostile threats, forced companies to supplement their food supply through hunting or cultivating vegetable gardens. These tasks were a burden on available personnel and prevented them from conducting training or fulfilling mission requirements.

The typical post was simply a collection of buildings focused on a central point, usually the parade ground. Few posts contained any measure of defensive works like a wooden stockade or stone wall, a reflection of the lack of determined Indian attempts to directly attack the post. With the exception of the rare Indian raid to capture horses or livestock, Plains Indian attacks on forts did not occur with any regularity. One post that did feature defensive fortification was Fort Phil Kearney in Wyoming. The post was built surrounded by an 800ft by 600ft wooden stockade, comprising 11ft pine logs set in a 3ft trench. Defensive works required additional materials and labor, and post commanders usually considered both commodities in short supply. In addition, if the post was only manned by a few companies and was temporary in nature, there was little reason to build permanent facilities.

Temporary posts consisted of a series of crude buildings that were built with available materials at hand such as adobe or rough-hewn logs. More permanent posts and forts were graced with buildings and quarters constructed with brick and intricate woodwork. Regardless of their temporary or permanent nature, all posts shared certain common facilities to ensure necessary functions were accomplished.

The main hub of activity was the post headquarters. A post commander, normally the senior officer present, presided over all operations. The post adjutant, normally a lieutenant, and a senior non-commissioned officer, a first-sergeant, assisted him in his administrative duties. These posts also had logistical requirements that were attended to by the assigned quartermaster sergeant. However, the quartermaster sergeant frequently required support, so

Post facilities gradually improved as the Plains Indian Wars subsided. These 1872 officer quarters at Fort Sill show a dramatic improvement over ones used in 1870. (RG95 Fort Sill Collection Box 8)

a soldier was detailed to perform as a clerk for supply management and accountability. A typical post contained a quartermaster warehouse that held all types of field equipment and supplies. Similarly, a commissary sergeant might need an assistant from a company to oversee the acquisition and preparation of food. Depending on the number of personnel at the post, the quartermaster, commissary, hospital, stables, and other facilities might need additional personnel to ensure smooth operations. Some companies, such as artillery units, might need an ordnance sergeant. The quartermaster, commissary, and ordnance sergeants were appointed from line unit non-commissioned officers. They were not counted as part of authorized company strength. The Army Regulations of 1861 specified that the Secretary of War could only select non-commissioned line officers with five years of service (three as a non-commissioned officer) to become ordnance (and in 1881 commissary) sergeants. By 1867, there were 112 ordnance and 146 commissary sergeants on active duty. However, most of the activities used to run the post were staffed by the company, which further reduced the combat effectiveness of the unit.

Isolated posts, like Camp Pilot Butte in Montana shown here in 1885, served as home to widely scattered units. A reliable water source was a key factor when considering where to locate a post. (RG24 Guy V. Henry .26)

Barracks were usually constructed to include open sleeping bays, a kitchen and mess room, a single washroom, a library (a luxury paid out of company funds), an armory, and offices for company administration handled by non-commissioned officers. The barracks usually had two floors with the sleeping quarters on the second floor. Officer quarters were more elegant and provided space for families. Typical post officer housing units were also two-story duplex buildings where officers had at least two bedrooms, a parlor, dining room, kitchen, and storage space. Commanding officers could have quarters with up to six bedrooms, a servant's room, parlor, dining room, and kitchen. The post might also contain a guardhouse, hospital, bachelor officer's quarters, quarters for non-commissioned officers and their families, chapel, wagon shop, stables, magazine, and other offices. If the post contained a cavalry unit, it would also feature a blacksmith shop, saddle shop, and hay yard.

Unofficial facilities were common. Some posts housed wives of enlisted personnel or civilian laundresses who cleaned clothing on "laundress row." The Army also allowed civilian traders to sell goods and merchandise on the post. Some of these "sutler stores" also sold alcoholic beverages, meals and ammunition. These sutlers received a franchise, and depending on the distance between the post and the nearest competition, could make a considerable amount of profit from underpaid officers, soldiers, their families, passing emigrants, the local populace—and reservation-Indians too. Army regulations forbade the sale of ammunition or arms to Indians though.

The sutler system came under attack from the War Department, which characterized it as "odious and demoralizing." The sutlers had a virtual monopoly on trade at many posts and forts. They were also exempt from any taxation since they operated on government property. The War Department eventually replaced these sutlers with a post exchange system on July 25, 1895.

Indian scouts and soldiers

The Army used Indian scouts throughout the campaign, exploiting inter-tribal animosity to gain Indian knowledge of local geography and other valuable information. Army commanders also organized auxiliary military units to support operations. Along with the tactical advantages offered by Indian service, the nation would gain by integrating them into wider American society through military service. Many Army and Bureau of Indian Affairs officials hoped that employing Indians to settle the West would aid their acceptance of the advance of "civilization."

Commanders such as George Crook praised these scouts for their expert horsemanship and tracking abilities that gave the Army a definite advantage in the field. These scouts were arranged into military units and were to prove a valuable resource on the Southern and Central Plains. From 1866–70, the Army used Pawnee scouts, which commanders reported as very successful. Crook used Crow and Shoshone Indian scouts in the 1876 Sioux campaign. Such scouts could negate any Indian advantage of mobility by keeping pace with them.

While some officers advocated the use of inter-tribal rivalries to motivate Indian scouts, Crook went one step further by promoting the idea of using Indians of the same tribe to scout and fight against fellow tribe members. He believed that seeing members of their own tribe fighting one another would demoralize hostile Indians. Crook used this technique in 1876 to fight the Sioux and employed it again in his campaigns against the Apaches in the Southwest.

The Army also used Indian auxiliaries to act as reservation police, which released Army units from guarding, monitoring, and maintaining law and order there. Additionally, Indian police could communicate and relate to tribal members better than Regular Army soldiers, diffusing potential conflicts.

By the early-1890s, the War Department was seriously exploring the idea of recruiting Indian soldiers into Regular Army regiments. War Department

General Orders No. 28 dated March 9, 1891 authorized the Army to recruit eight troops of cavalry and 19 companies of Indians. These companies were to be commanded by white officers and eventually staffed with Indian non-commissioned officers. In September 1891, Schofield reported seven companies of Indian troops were fully manned, with nine more companies in the process of recruitment.

Critics complained bitterly. Some officers argued that Indians were uncivilized and unable to train as useful soldiers, others believed that relying on Indians to spy on and kill their own was unrealistic. Additionally, many opponents objected to the Army's treatment of Indians through forcing them into an organization that would strip them of their individuality. Still others argued that language and cultural differences were too wide a gap to bridge and their effectiveness and efficiency would not compare to white units. The arguments resulted in Indian scout billets remaining unfilled. Unfortunately, Philip Sheridan also opposed the use of Indians as scouts and auxiliaries as soldiers when he was Commanding General of the Army. He believed they would find and coax Indians to return to the reservation, but not kill their brethren.

Many of these arguments were countered by events in the field. Commanders who used Indian scouts observed that the scouts rarely deserted; they were effective in finding their enemies; and they even helped to defend soldiers and fight against other tribes. Critics of Indian scouts and auxiliaries continued to press their concerns over their use into the 1890s. Many of their arguments were also used against African-American cavalry and infantry regiments who served well in the field, even though their units were undermanned and short of equipment. The Army's effectiveness in the field would have been severely affected if Indian scouts and auxiliaries were abolished. Congress would also have had to allocate more soldiers to the Plains to increase patrols and to staff posts.

This photograph shows a typical Indian scout and his family. The scout wears an Army dress uniform helmet. (RG485 E.S. Godfrey .314)

Army Indian scouts provided invaluable service on the Plains. Shaplish was one of those who chose to help the Army against fellow braves. (RG126 W.C. Brown .201)

Tactics

The Army made a distinction between strategy and tactics. The War Department defined strategy as the art of handling or moving soldiers out of sight of the enemy or at a distance from the enemy, for example in the use of converging columns or winter campaigns. The focus of strategy was to place units into a position that improved the chances of defeating the enemy or reduce the risk of defeat. Army officers defined tactics as maneuvering or employing troops in the presence or immediate vicinity of the enemy, with special emphasis on the battlefield.

The Army further subdivided tactics into minor and grand tactics. Minor tactics concentrated on the use of small numbers of soldiers that were from the same arm or branch. Grand tactics broadened the scope of operations to include situations where more than one arm or branch conducted operations, and the handling of armies in, or about to do, battle. Cavalry, infantry, and artillery commanders were schooled in maneuver and fighting tactics. Maneuver tactics involved the use of particular movements to position soldiers to prepare for battle. Fighting tactics were concerned with the procedures, formations, and actions necessary to attack or defend against an opponent. War Department period handbooks indicated that maneuver tactics served as a key link with strategy. Strategy involved maneuver and movements between a campaign area and a particular field of battle—movements that used the same formations and instruction as maneuver tactics. War Department officials believed that officers and enlisted men could learn maneuver tactics from a thorough understanding and practice of drill regulations. However, fighting tactics required more flexibility and consideration of the environment and situation.

Regimental and company commanders were especially interested in tactics since they had to implement field movement and fighting procedures. These commanders needed to have a firm understanding of maneuver due to the geographical separation of regiments and the lack of inter-company training throughout the period. Similarly, non-commissioned officers' responsibilities included training their squads and sections to ensure they followed the proper procedures and instructions to fight the enemy.

Not all officers believed that tactical study was valuable. Opponents, such as Capt. James Chester in 1886, expressed the opinion that reliance on fixed tactics was similar to dogma and would "poison" the minds of junior officers and rob them of initiative. Other officers merely dismissed any tactical innovations since the United States had already gathered sufficient lessons from the Civil War: the real issue was seacoast fortification and repelling any

The government established Indian agencies in desolate locations. This encampment was photographed near the Red Cloud Agency, Wyoming Territory in 1870. (RG315 Daughters of the US Army .453)

invasion of the nation. For them Indian warfare required no new tactics, just modifications of existing ones. Besides, some officers thought, soldiers in the field had little time to devote to tactical study since they were busy maintaining their posts, on patrol, or fighting Indians.

Nelson Miles and his staff view the large, "hostile" Indian camp near Pine Ridge, South Dakota, on January 16, 1891. The Pine Ridge campaign ended the Plains Indian Wars. (RG262S Indian Wars Collection .31)

Tactical influences

During the period of the Plains Indian Wars, officer education, be it on the banks of West Point's Hudson River, or through the tactical handbooks available to volunteer officers, stressed tactics suitable for massed armies in Europe.

The Army had been in thrall to French military ideas from uniforms to tactics during the Civil War. West Point graduates who had ascended to the highest positions within Army leadership had been schooled in the philosophy of war espoused by Henri Jomini, an officer on Napoleon Bonaparte's staff, which dominated much of the tactics curriculum at the United States Military Academy. For example, one of Jomini's fundamental principles was: "To maneuver to engage fractions of the hostile army with the bulk of ones' forces." The Union Army of the Potomac, under George McClellan, spent much of its early campaigns in a strategy to outmaneuver Confederate forces and create conditions where they could dominate their opponent in a decisive engagement. Winfield Scott, William J. Hardee, and Silas Casey had all written tactics and drill manuals that officers widely read and studied for the Civil War, based on European military thought. Unfortunately, many of the tactics they suggested proved fatal or ineffective in the Civil War.

This diagram shows how Army units protected a main column through the use of advance guards, flankers, and rear guards.

The Civil War had witnessed the beginning of a revolution in military operations. Breech-loading rifles, the railroad, the telegraph, and other military innovations forced many officers to question the relevance of established tactics. Frontal attacks against entrenched defenses had ended with bloody losses for Union and Confederate forces on the offensive. Rifled weaponry from small arms to artillery had made these little more than suicidal. Reformers such as Sherman and Sheridan demanded the development of tactics appropriate for the American battlefield, rather than those appropriate for operations in Europe.

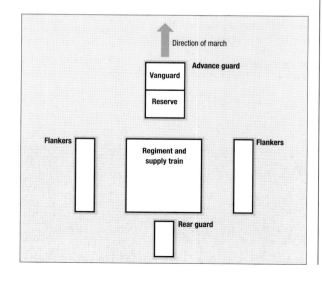

Direction of march

Advance guard

Vanguard

Reserve

Flankers

Regiment and supply train

Flankers

Rear guard

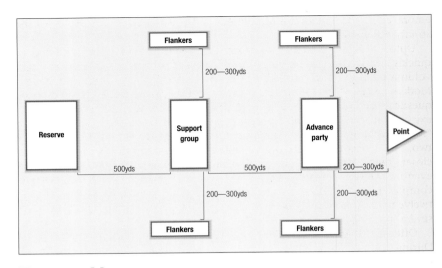

Emory Upton

One of the post-war army's most vocal critics and innovative officers, Emory Upton, took on the challenge to rewrite a tactical manual. Sherman was enthralled with Upton's observations. Eventually, Emory Upton would become the Commandant of Cadets at West Point and teach tactics there. Upton's dissatisfaction with the written advice from Hardee and Casey along with his Civil War experience gave him the motivation to draft his book, *A New System of Infantry Tactics, Double and Single Rank*. Modern firepower and the slavish devotion to following obsolete tactics, like those of Hardee, produced slaughter on the battlefield. Emory Upton proposed tactics that would allow the conduct of operations, but without the horrendous casualties of the Civil War. Modern weapons replaced massed volley fire and the reliance on multiple columns.

Upton sought to reduce the target size of an Army unit through diffusion and the reliance upon greater firepower from troops. In addition, he stressed the use of skirmishers to protect columns. His tactics encouraged commanders to use fewer forces and apply maneuver to accomplish missions that traditionally relied on much larger contingents of troops. Firepower reduced the need for volleys of muskets and forced officers to use new methods to reduce their own vulnerability to breech-loading rifles. The War Department agreed to review Upton's concepts and two committees eventually adopted them, after intensive study. Grant oversaw one committee and significantly helped Upton's work become the official Army tactics manual on August 1, 1867.

Although Emory Upton concentrated on infantry tactics, his influence on the Army affected all branches. Upton advocated a series of tactics that would find universal application among the infantry, artillery, and cavalry. The Army adopted this program of "assimilated" tactics, which translated into a series of common commands and formations that officers could employ across branches. Upton designed these tactics to be used as shared concepts, not as combined arms tactics. However, the War Department saw these tactics as a device to allow officers in one branch to operate with those of other branches with common terms and methodology. Additionally, officers who transferred between branches could more easily adapt to their assignments given this common background.

Sherman insisted that Upton continue his work on tactics. The War Department authorized the publication of three separate handbooks for the infantry, cavalry, and artillery throughout the period. Secretary of War William Belknap effectively made Upton's tactics official Army policy when he signed War Department General Order, No. 6, dated July 17, 1873. This order provided official acceptance of the tactics for regular and militia units. Specifically, the order ensured uniformity, stating "all exercises, evolutions, and ceremonies not embraced in the Tactics are prohibited, and those therein prescribed will be strictly observed."

Upton recognized that breech-loading rifles and rapid-fire artillery would quickly leave close formations riddled with casualties. The accuracy and volume of fire had improved from the Napoleonic to the Civil War period. Modern breech-loading rifles in the post-Civil War period created more questions about infantry tactics. His tactics recommended two changes to existing tactical formations. The Army should use infantry formations based on "fours" and implement a reduction of multiple rank formations to only one or two. The concept of fours would enable men to react to new situations under closer, more effective supervision. Upton envisioned this organization to eventually replace squads, sections, and platoons, which never occurred. Units composed of fours, like a company, would have several squads of eight to twelve men. Although Upton's ideas seemed to look good on paper, there were several points of criticism.

Officers believed the "fours" organization would break under pressure. During combat, as casualties mounted, soldiers were supposed to reorganize themselves into new groups of four. In the heat of battle, the ability of soldiers to fight and to reorganize was doubtful at best. Command and control would break down without direct leadership to force soldiers to regroup. Most critics thought the system worked only on the parade ground. Additionally, some units might not be divisible by four and there would be problems dealing with the one or two soldiers that could not form a "four" to maneuver or fight.

Upton also suggested that infantry units fight as one rank, two at the most. Rifles allowed infantrymen to provide a mass of firing that did not require more than two ranks. Additionally, forming a company into more than two ranks offered a very lucrative target to enemy formations with rifles or artillery. A single rank of infantry or dismounted cavalry allowed it to move faster, and react to situations more quickly. A second rank could support the first or become another formation able to fight independently of the first. Officers thus had more flexibility to deploy their infantry companies or appropriate units to react swiftly in a fluid situation.

Several officers disapproved of Upton's assumptions concerning an assimilated system, claiming he disregarded the unique characteristics of each branch. Other officers argued that infantry organization and tactics differed considerably from those of cavalry or artillery. Forcing officers to use common organization, commands, and tactics would stifle innovation and might even impact on a unit's effectiveness. Although several Army officers proposed their own systems of tactics to replace Upton's, the War Department did not seriously entertain updating Upton's work until 1888. Throughout most of the Plains Indian Wars, officers and men trained and organized according to Emory Upton's work.

At the urging of Emory Upton, Army marksmanship programs expanded throughout the service. These men, armed with single-shot Springfield rifles, could provide accurate, long-range firepower. (RG113 M.F. Steele .145)

Upton's published works

Emory Upton's works concentrated on minor tactics, and he did not address grand tactics or combined arms: he was also not averse to criticizing current Army training policies. The War Department printed the infantry, cavalry, and artillery tactics handbooks with the same commands and illustrations throughout, reflecting the attempt to unify these branches under Upton's assimilated system. Depending on the branch handbook, tactics also focused on unique "schools" of instruction. For the soldier of the 1870s, many of the tactics were irrelevant or only applicable for drill or if the unit defended a major city that was located away from the frontier. However, officers and men did not cast aside all of Upton's tactics. Army commanders used many of Upton's tactical suggestions on maneuver to protect columns. This emphasis was especially valuable in protecting wagon trains, supply convoys, or other moving columns.

Upton's original text on infantry tactics, written in 1867 and revised in 1873, provided the reader with a host of commands and recommended tactical maneuvers. His *United States Army Infantry Tactics* from 1877 begins with the "School of the Soldier" and builds in succeeding chapters to tactics for hypothetical brigades and divisions. The "School of the Soldier" concerns itself with training an individual soldier to conduct individual movements, facings, manual of arms, firing commands, reloading procedures, bayonet drill, and other activities.

One example of Upton's reforms dealt with individual target practice. Field commanders faced shortages of ammunition from 1865 to the late-1870s. Some infantry units, such as the 18th Infantry in 1866, eliminated target practice because of the lack of ammunition. Upton sought to improve this military necessity through a standard practice program. Annually, Upton recommended, at a minimum, that men fire ten rounds each at targets at ranges of 100, 150, 200, 250, 300, 350, and 400 yards. He recommended next that soldiers were to fire five live rounds at targets 500, 600, 700, and 800 yards away. Army officers should also allocate an additional 40 rounds to fire in squad, platoon, and company formations and maneuvers. Upton also encouraged individual soldiers, especially new recruits or soldiers, to prepare and shoot 60 rounds before going on any campaign to acclimatize themselves to gunfire and their weapons. Upton recognized the need for improved marksmanship to increase and improve Army firepower: unfortunately, the War Department placed more emphasis on cost savings and budget reductions. Generally, Civil War musketry required volumes of firepower, but little expert marksmanship. However, the improved accuracy of rifles meant that these weapons could strike targets at great distances, but they required consistent marksmanship practice. Upton's efforts eventually forced the Army leadership to expand the authorized ammunition for target practice.

Indian tribes lived nomadic lives and, sometimes, had the same or better weapons than the Army. Of major concern to Army officers was tribal mobility, but they countered this by conducting winter campaigns. (RG113 M.F. Steele .135)

Convoy and escort tactics

Upton's infantry tactics and other branch tactics for companies and higher organizations concentrated on maneuver. "The School of the Company" , for infantry and cavalry stressed the use of advance, flanking, and rear guards to protect the movements of columns or convoys. The Army had used soldiers to protect the head, flanks, and rear of a column throughout the Civil War. Army officers had to use these tactics with greater emphasis during the Plains Indian Wars. Army officers used advance guards to reconnoiter the area ahead of a column, cover its movement, prevent surprise attack, and protect it from an ambush. If a column was driving towards an objective, then the advance guard could also seize and hold positions or sustain contact with the enemy until the main column could launch its attack. Similarly, in retreat, the advance guard also prepared the ground in front of the column, capturing key positions or sweeping the area of the enemy. Army officers deploying an advance guard split the unit into two parts: the vanguard and support elements. The column's commander further divided the vanguard into an advance party and a support element. The advance party formed leading and flanking groups while the support element had its own flankers.

The instructions on how to form an advance group contain much detail. Upton recommended that an advance group consist of one-eighth (for smaller units) to a quarter (for larger ones) of the total force. Within the advance guard's vanguard, the lead elements comprised a point (or lead) group and flanking groups. A corporal and four privates made up the point with flanking groups of three to four men in support. The advance guard commander normally placed the point and flanking groups about 200–300 yards from the main advance party. Additionally, the commander of the advance guard also used small detachments of two to three men, each at an interval, to keep in contact with the support group.

The vanguard's support group with its flankers traveled behind the advance party by 500 yards. The vanguard's commander generally stayed with the support group. The advance guard also had a reserve, approximately half of the advance guard, within 500 yards of the support group. The advance guard's commander stayed with the reserve.

The rear guard had a similar composition to that of the advance guard. However, the rear guard's strength was about half the size of the advance guard. It protected the column from raiding parties, arrested any stragglers, and stopped any pillaging. The rear guard would protect the column in retreat and delay the enemy while the bulk of the column maneuvered.

Some examples of the advance flanking and rear guards in use might include cavalry units protecting a wagon train or infantrymen watching over a railroad construction crew. During a regimental movement in 1868, the 7th Cavalry used these guards to protect the regiment and its supply train on the Arkansas River. Custer also used this tactic to protect the main regiment and supply train. The flanking guard commanders positioned their forces within 500 yards of the main column body. These commanders also kept their soldiers within not more than half a mile from the advance and rear guards. Unfortunately, the use of such guards accounted for a great amount of assigned regimental forces. The 7th Cavalry only had twelve companies, with eight on guard. Officers could use these guards to fend off Indian surprise attacks, but if the Indians made an attack on the main column, then reforming the regiment to defend or counterattack would take time.

Army policy also dictated that units perform escort duty for civilian wagon trains, stagecoaches, survey parties, or mail carriers. These escort missions ordinarily required not more than a company; however, depending on the size or value of the convoy, the escort could expand. The escort would use the same concept of advanced, flanking, and rear guards. In addition, an escort might use an advance cavalry element that scouted up to five miles ahead of the convoy. This advance cavalry component could send patrols out to gather intelligence and locate the enemy. If the cavalry patrols discovered hostile Indians, the escort commander could divert the wagon train away from this threat. Depending on the size of the Indian raiding party, a cavalry patrol might disperse the braves. Otherwise, Army policy directed the advance cavalry not commit to an offensive engagement, but instead defend against and observe the enemy. The advance cavalry unit's primary responsibility was to collect specific information about the composition, strength, intent, and location of the enemy. Advanced cavalry units did not provide convoy security as their principal mission.

Escort duty had specific requirements. The Army used the standard of approximately two infantrymen per wagon and one cavalryman per eight wagons, which in a convoy of 50 to 60 wagons would require an extensive commitment. Once under military escort, the escort commander (who, by regulation, had to be a commissioned officer) took command of the entire movement and directed the time of march, order, and encampments. Normally, the company and its escort traveled no more than 25 miles a day.

The escort commander's mission was to hold the enemy at bay while allowing the convoy and its escort to continue its journey. If the military escort could not keep Indian attackers at a safe distance from the convoy, then soldiers took defensive measures to protect the train. Escort commanders typically assigned the bulk of their military strength to the main body as a central reserve to act swiftly in a defensive manner. When commanders could not protect their escorts or when the defensive measures failed, they would order any assets unable to escape by flight to be destroyed. Drill regulations directed: "animals must be taken away or shot."

Convoys were sometimes difficult to defend. Wagons did not travel at a uniform speed or for the same duration. If escort commanders allowed the wagon train to form as a column with wagons in single file, then travel discipline might fall apart. A long convoy might cause individual wagons and the escort to separate along the travel path, allowing Indian raiding parties to overwhelm any limited military protection and pick off wagons individually. Instead, approved Army tactics urged wagons, depending on the geography and number, to form abreast, to concentrate them and allow for better travel discipline and defense. Conversely, if the wagon train was too concentrated, Indians might capture or destroy a part of the wagon train or convoy before any military escort could react. If the escorting military forces came under Indian attack, then the commander must make the defense "as severe and bloody as possible, in order to teach them a wholesome respect for the convoy escorts." This request assumed that officers had sufficient men to conduct a counterattack.

Army commanders also needed to protect convoys and wagon trains during their transit through narrow passes. The convoy might have to pass in single file and a commander might not have room to send reinforcements to defend an attacked convoy. Before entering an area where the convoy or wagon train might travel under dangerous conditions, the commander needed to conduct extensive reconnaissance to detect any chance of an ambush. If successful, the advance guard rapidly moved through the pass or defile. The advance guard would then form a defensive position well away from the pass exit to allow the convoy to park its vehicles in a corral as they left the defile. Depending on the situation, a commander might send the entire column through the pass. If the convoy was too large, then the escort commander evenly divided it. The front or first half, which led the convoy, halted at the entrance of the pass. Officers led the rear or second half as quickly as possible through the defile, exited, and then parked its vehicles where it could rest, feed, and water the convoy's animals. The front half then transited the narrow passage and assumed the lead of the convoyed vehicles as it left the defile.

Most Indian families moved across the Plains almost effortlessly. This family is able to carry its tee-pee and possessions on a single travois. (RG485 E.S. Godfrey .273)

Skirmishers

Upton suggested that Army officers use skirmishers to "clear the way for the main body." The *United States Army Infantry Tactics* handbook suggested that officers use a company of skirmishers for regimental-sized engagements. Upton wrote that a commander needed to keep a distance of five yards between each man. However, most commanders were content to keep a line of skirmishers within sight of each other. Men could vary the distance to suit vegetation and cover. Additionally, the column should not deploy the entire selected company in line as skirmishers. Instead, the company commander needed to keep some non-commissioned and other ranks in reserve to plug gaps and maintain contact with the skirmishers to gather reports and supply ammunition. If the Indians attacked the skirmishers, then the deployed troops, on command, would form a circle at a rally point and defend themselves. Once the danger had passed, the skirmishers would return to their positions.

Field commanders could use a single company or more to deploy skirmishers on the right and left wings. Upton recommended that commanders have the option to deploy skirmishers in depth. Soldiers could form up to three lines, depending on the number of men used in this capacity, at varying distance from the main column.

Skirmishers allowed commanders the flexibility to conduct a number of operations. If the Army was using converging columns, a line of skirmishers, in a loose formation using infantrymen or dismounted cavalry deployed abreast, could be used as a screen to block the advance or retreat of Indians until the main attack force caught up with the line. Commanders could also use skirmishers to catch the enemy in a surprise move, particularly useful in rough terrain. Although Indian warriors did not have the disciplined firepower of trained infantry, frequently individual braves had repeating rifles that produced a higher volume of fire compared to that of the individual soldier. The use of skirmishers reduced this threat by avoiding massed formations.

Upton believed that soldiers should arrive in columns on a battlefield, reducing its size as a target by moving quickly head-on and allowing it to mass on a critical position. Upton suggested skirmishers arrive within 150 yards of an enemy position. As the advancing main column got closer to the enemy, a commander could then add more soldiers to the skirmish line. When the main column was within 200 yards of the enemy, the column's commander would then issue an order to maneuver from column to a line. The use of a line allowed the Army to use its firepower to inflict maximum damage on a foe.

Common fighting tactics

Upton's tactics were best suited to fighting forces armed with breech-loading rifles or light artillery. The Indians did not have such weapons nor did they fight with a centralized command and control system. Had they done so, they would have overwhelmed the small forts and posts within the Division of the Missouri. Field commanders used particular tactics with regularity throughout the period. Despite the lack of official Indian warfare doctrine, Army officers and men used several common tactics to fight and defend. One of the most common tactics was the surprise attack. Aside from using converging columns and winter campaigns in an overall strategy, commanders used attacks at dawn or early in the morning. Officers conducting a dawn attack usually found Indian tribes ill prepared to conduct a vigorous defense. Additionally, dawn attacks allowed the Army to maneuver unnoticed during darkness.

Company and regimental commanders could also opt to attack on the spur of the moment, and in a lightning strike. The cavalry's mobility provided a definite advantage in this type of operation, whereas the infantry presented the commander with the ability to hit the Indians with accurate, relatively high rates of rifle fire that could decimate a tribe caught by the cavalry's action. This type of attack relied on individual commander initiative. Split-second decision-making was required, and the attack relied on the formation's mass and speed

Passing through a defilade or narrow pass was not an insurmountable task. The Army used advance and rear guards, as demonstrated in the five stages of this diagram.

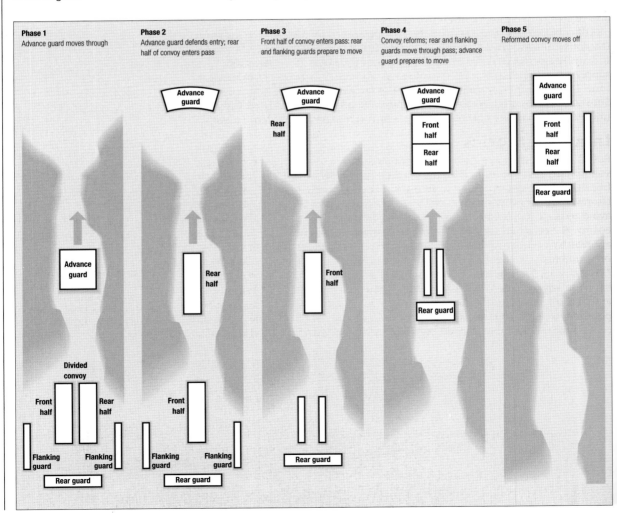

Phase 1
Advance guard moves through

Phase 2
Advance guard defends entry; rear half of convoy enters pass

Phase 3
Front half of convoy enters pass; rear and flanking guards prepare to move

Phase 4
Convoy reforms; rear and flanking guards move through pass; advance guard prepares to move

Phase 5
Reformed convoy moves off

to strike a decisive blow, as well as adequate intelligence about an enemy. Without this, it could end up in disaster, as happened to Custer at Little Big Horn. Additionally, if the commander did not properly plan the attack, elements of the attacking force could lose contact and coordination with other parts of the command.

Planned attacks required intelligence gathering, preparation, and enough forces to conduct a well-coordinated assault. If a commander could maneuver into proper position, have sufficient force, use surprise, and speed, then he could make the attack an overwhelming success. Unfortunately, the Plains Indians were mobile and if they spotted Army units preparing for this they would quickly disperse. The planned attack worked best against "fixed" targets such as winter camps.

Army units were not always on the offensive. Commanders at times required troops to defend themselves after an ambush or an abortive assault. The combined battalions of Maj. Marcus Reno and Capt. Frederick Benteen successfully repelled an attack of Sioux forces during the Little Big Horn campaign. Reno was able to rally his soldiers after an aborted attack on the main Sioux camp. He formed a circular defensive position behind equipment and fallen horses. Dismounted cavalrymen and infantry could also form lines to concentrate fire to break the attack of Indians. Archeological evidence from the Little Big Horn battlefield indicates that companies formed defensive lines to slow the advance of Indian braves against the ill-fated Custer battalion. They also formed a "V" formation during Custer's last stand.

Officers also had the opportunity to retreat or withdraw. If a commander faced a significant threat, he could decline further enemy contact. After Sioux Indians had discovered and attacked his column, George Crook retreated to his supply base. Crook's column, one of three of the Little Big Horn campaign in June 1876, was unavailable to support any later attacks by Custer. Crow and Shoshone scouts stopped Sioux and Cheyenne attacks and allowed Crook to muster several cavalry charges to these well co-ordinated and intense assaults.

Infantry tactics

Post-Civil War infantry tactics concentrated on how to overcome precise, voluminous rifle fire from an entrenched position when attacking. Fortunately, frontier officers did not have to face these conditions fighting Plains Indians. However, officers and men generally used dispersion in attack and defense to avoid accurate fire. Infantry officers used a combination of methods to attack the enemy. A commander could order fire by company, wing, or rank. For example, an infantry battalion commander (assuming there was more than one company on campaign) would give the commands "Fire by company," "Battalion," "Ready," and, finally, "Commence Firing." The company at the far right of the battalion began the procedure with the commands "Company," "Aim," "Fire," and "Load" (ready for the next fire command). The company to the left then prepared to fire, and so on until ordered to stop. Similarly, the battalion commander could allow companies to instruct individual soldiers to fire at will.

These infantrymen have formed a typical skirmish-line deployment: this tactical demonstration is taking place on the Little Big Horn battlefield in 1886. (RG 48 Edward S. Godfrey 2.3)

A typical infantry skirmish line. Infantry units could deploy in this way to avoid concentrated fire.

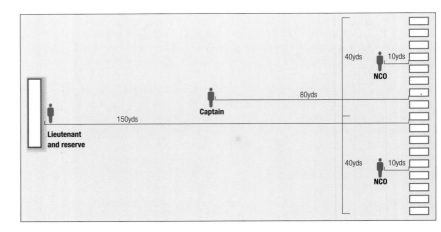

Commanders could also charge by column, as demonstrated in this diagram. One platoon column would follow the first.

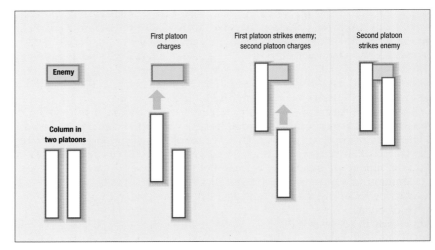

Emory Upton's key influence on Army tactics was advising officers to organize their soldiers into "fours," as illustrated by these infantrymen. (RG 48 Edward S. Godfrey 2.4)

Plains Indians were adept at surprise ambushes. Infantrymen needed to rely on discipline and training. Unfortunately, the lack of fully trained recruits, few available soldiers, and a minimal marksmanship program produced infantrymen who were ill prepared to handle combat operations in the field. Upton had stressed that officers needed to develop soldiers able to take the individual initiative to act as a skirmisher and assess tactical situations. Unfortunately, when infantrymen did form and fire against Indians, the enemy

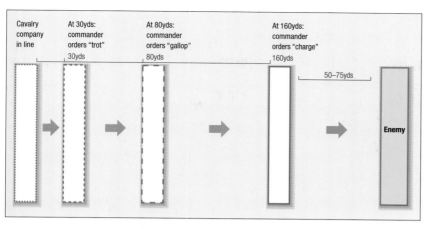

| Cavalry company in line | At 30yds: commander orders "trot" | At 80yds: commander orders "gallop" | At 160yds: commander orders "charge" | | Enemy |

Cavalry commanders who ordered a charge would gradually increase the speed of their advance until the unit struck the enemy.

usually did not stand and meet the Army. Infantry officers did not have the mobility to conclude a successful charge, bayonet or not, if the enemy were mobile. With the exception of a few instances, there were few pitched battles where infantry could use their firepower and prevail on the battlefield.

Cavalry tactics

Infantry and cavalry tactics were similar in philosophy and execution. Since dismounted cavalry fought like the infantry, many of the maneuvers and fighting tactics were the same. Dismounted carbine and revolver fire was more accurate than firing when mounted. Additionally, soldiers on horses made good targets. The cavalry's value was in its ability to rapidly conduct a series of holding, supporting or attacking actions.

Common mounted tactics included moving from column to a line, conducting route marches, or forming a column or wheel. However, the true value of cavalry, noted in several period documents, was in its shock tactics, particularly the cavalry charge.

Despite Hollywood's glorification of the cavalry charge, few units used their sabers on campaign, let alone in combat. Sabers were additional weight for the overloaded cavalryman, and they could create "giveaway" noise if they struck other equipment that would alert the enemy to their presence. Instead, cavalrymen used their carbines and revolvers, usually dismounted, though they did occasionally conduct mounted attacks. Undulating terrain, without obstacles like trees, was best for a charge. Level terrain allowed the enemy to see the charge and a clear field of fire.

Officers were urged to order a cavalry charge only over short distances, in order to keep good control and not to fatigue the horses. A cavalry officer conducted a typical charge by forming his unit into a line, normally from a column. The line advanced from a slow walk, to a trot, then a gallop, and finally the charge. The distance between the start of the charge (when officers and men drew their weapons) and contact with the enemy was optimally 50 to 75 yards. A commander also needed to keep a small reserve from the charge to protect his own flanks or strike the enemy's. If the attack succeeded, the commanding officer was not to allow the enemy to rally, but instead force him from the field. If the charge did break through the enemy lines, the commanding officer could rally his soldiers, and then turn around and charge the enemy again.

One drawback of charging in line was that it offered a wide front with little depth and might not have sufficient force to break the enemy's defenses. The alternative was to charge in a column, perhaps performing several column attacks successively to break through at a particular point. The disadvantage of this was that it exposed large flanks. The protect these, the commander might form a double column.

Cavalrymen in a defensive circle using their mounts as temporary barriers. Officers frequently fought dismounted in both offensive and defensive operations. (RG488 S.B. Young .68)

Artillery tactics

Artillery did not play a dominant role in the Plains Indian Wars. The principal offensive mission for the artillery was to support the attacks of the other branches. When in a defensive position, an artillery unit's objective was to break-up any assault. Artillery tactics were relatively straightforward cannons and other pieces always fought on line and traveled in column Artillery units were located at departmental headquarters, at forts, or on Indian reservations and agencies, often guarding or protecting fortifications The Army assigned only a few artillery companies to Plains posts. Most of the artillery units were stationed in the Department of the Platte or the Missouri The Department of Dakota rarely had permanently stationed artillery units within its area of operations.

On campaign, artillery could disperse concentrations of Indians: its ability to destroy a target up to 3,000 yards away presented a commander with a useful tool. Some officers raised questions over its value though. Expeditionary commanders used artillery on several campaigns, such as the Sioux campaign in 1876 and Wounded Knee during the Ghost Dance campaign in 1891. Like the cavalry officer, the artillery officer followed tactics based on maneuver and combat formation. Upton's assimilated tactical system, as already noted provided common formations, commands, and maneuvers that other branch officers would comprehend and use. Few artillery units actually deployed into the field. Instead, infantry and cavalry soldiers manned and operated artillery pieces, Gatling guns, and howitzers, not artillery units. Horses considered unfit for cavalry service normally drew the caissons to transport the weapon.

Army officers could execute fire to their front; at an angle to the enemy line in enfilade from a position on the enemy's flanks; or in crossfire from separate positions. Commanders could also engage direct fire (at a target within sight) indirect fire (at a concealed or obscured target), or reverse fire (to strike at positions in the enemy's rear.) To avoid presenting too easy a target, officer kept a spacing of at least ten yards between artillery pieces.

If the artillery succeeded in disrupting the enemy, the infantry and cavalry could then quickly attack. If the infantry or cavalry offensive failed, the gunners had to concentrate maximum firepower against the enemy, to allow the infantry or cavalry to regroup. If the infantry or cavalry broke through the enemy positions, an artillery commander's first action was to move all of the pieces to the captured position and support the infantry and cavalry's flanks.

Commanders seldom used artillery in isolation, as crew members armed with revolvers could barely defend themselves or their artillery pieces from a nearby enemy. Commanders placed infantry support with the artillery piece while the cavalry reserves posted themselves in the rear and on the flanks.

Weapons and equipment

Restricted budgets and a vast surplus of aging Civil War-era weapons and equipment plagued the United States Army throughout the duration of the Plains Indian Wars. The Ordnance Department did introduce new weapons (such as the Gatling gun) and modify old weapons to incorporate new technology, but this was painfully slow. Warehouses filled with surplus weapons provided a mountain of spare parts that flooded the system and influenced a cost-saving Congress. The Army's use of particular weapons certainly affected the way soldiers deployed and fought. The Army was at a disadvantage with this inflexible system that inhibited the acquisition of modern rifles, such as repeating ones.

The improvements seemed marginal in comparison to commercially available weapons for civilians or Indians. For example, while the Winchester repeating rifle was a standard weapon throughout the West, infantry soldiers used breech-loading, single-shot rifles that the Army had modified well after 1865 from Civil War muskets.

Infantry weapons

The main weapon for infantrymen in the period was the shoulder rifle. The Union Army had used Springfield rifled muskets during the Civil War, which were relatively slow to reload and accurate at only short ranges. The rifled musket used a paper cartridge that contained a Minié ball (a shaped bullet) and powder charge. A percussion cap under the weapon's hammer ignited the paper cartridge.

The Army did experiment with modified Springfield weapons that were breech-loading and accepted a .58-cal. metal cartridge, but the cartridge was underpowered and its extractor proved deficient. However, these experiments showed promise. The metallic cartridge allowed soldiers to store and use ammunition in damp conditions and it was sturdier than the paper cartridge. The Ordnance Department converted several Springfield rifled muskets into the models 1865 and 1866 as experiments, and these modified rifles became the standard weapon used by the typical infantryman up to 1873. The Army would use this rifle and the Model 1873 Springfield version throughout the Plains Indian Wars until a magazine-fed Krag-Jorgensen rifle replaced it in 1892.

The "Long Tom" or trapdoor Springfield rifle was the invention of Erskin S. Allin, an armorer at the US Government's Springfield Arsenal in Massachusetts. He submitted a proposal to change the .58-cal. weapon to use a .50-cal. metallic cartridge. The rifle required a new barrel and it allowed a trained infantryman to fire about 13 rounds per minute versus three for the rifled musket, well above Civil War standards. The new Springfield's range also doubled to about 600 yards. These changes in technology, as noted previously, forced a review in tactics, as massed formations were sitting ducks. The long-range rifles created few situations where infantrymen on the Plains could use a bayonet. Like the cavalrymen's saber, the Army ignored the bayonet on the frontier.

The added firepower allowed the infantry to repulse many determined Indian attacks. For example, on August 2, 1867, 27 soldiers and four civilians from the 27th Infantry Regiment, under Capt. James W. Powell,

Although this photograph shows army soldiers in the Modoc War (Northern California) in 1872, it illustrates period uniforms and weapons. Note the Springfield carbine held by the soldier on the right. (RG 262S Indian Wars Collection .42)

This company from the 7th Infantry, armed with Springfield rifles, prepares to take the field against the Sioux in the Pine Ridge campaign in 1890. The infantry continued to use Springfields until 1891. (RG315 Daughters of the US Army .394)

defended themselves against about 1,000 Sioux braves. The Sioux had previously observed that soldiers were limited to a first volley and then had to slowly reload their muskets. The braves could then shower the troops with arrows and charge their positions. The soldiers, defending from a series of wagons, formed in a corral. The Indians killed six soldiers and wounded two others. However, the "Long Toms" allowed the infantrymen to present fierce return fire that resulted in the deaths of 60 braves and 120 wounded. The new rifles provided a distinct advantage over the Indians using arrows, lances, and surplus muskets.

The Army started to equip infantry units with the new Springfield rifle, but some units continued to employ the rifled musket and some seven-shot Spencer and Sharps .52-cal. percussion rifles. The Spencer was very popular with the cavalry in its carbine version. Unfortunately, it used a .50/60-cal. cartridge, incompatible with the Springfield's use of a .50/70-cal. round. The Army's drive to standardize weapons forced infantry units to accept the Springfield rifle: it started to issue the Springfield to all units when the Model 1868 was in full production.

The Army satisfied Congressional economic concerns by using the model 1866 and 1868 Springfield rifles. In 1869, Sherman convened a board of officers, the Schofield Board, to review Upton's assimilated tactics, but added the responsibility of evaluating small arms to determine the best rifles, carbines, and pistols. Arms manufacturers flocked to push their weapons, but not the least concern was the Ordnance Department's desire to continue Springfield rifle production. The small arms debate was controversial. The Army formed a second board, the Terry Board, and it adopted the Springfield Model 1873 with which it would eventually arm all infantrymen. The Model 1873 had an improved long-range sight (up to 1,100 yards), was better built and weighed less than its predecessors.

The Terry Board wanted to increase the rate of fire of rifles. The board had decided to adopt a .45/70-cal. cartridge to standardize ammunition among all small arms. The .45-cal. round gave a soldier with a Springfield rifle an effective range of about 600 yards. The Winchester repeater's range was about 200 yards and it had a slower reloading time. The board could not find a rifle that provided an adequate magazine or was rugged enough for the frontier.

The Army had to evaluate a number of other considerations when it chose a standard rifle. One benefit of the Springfield rifle was its relative simplicity and the fact that it was a proven weapon. The Army's long logistical tail had to supply parts to replace broken, worn, or defective mechanisms. Most of the soldiers on the Plains were not trained gunsmiths and the Springfield was easier to maintain in the field. The rifle could also withstand the rigors of frontier service. In the early 1870s, many of the new recruits were foreign born and had little technical knowledge let alone mastery of English.

One problem that plagued the Army was the jamming of ammunition in breech-loading weapons. After firing a rifle or carbine, the soldier had to extract the spent metallic cartridge. If not continually cleaned, the metallic cartridges would react chemically when the copper casings and the shell were exposed to leather treated with tannic acid. The Ordnance Department had originally given the soldier a leather cartridge box and belt. A greenish substance, verdigris, would form on the shell and, when heated from firing, would fuse the spent casing to the firing chamber. Soldiers had to use a knife to dig out the spent cartridge, which slowed or halted firing, a deadly condition on the Plains. Individual soldiers started to carry their ammunition in canvas belts. Eventually the Army changed its equipment policy, and it salvaged the leather cartridge belts and encased them in canvas with canvas loops to store rounds.

Cavalry weapons

Cavalrymen used three primary weapons: a carbine, a revolver, and a saber. Like the infantry, the cavalry suffered from post-Civil War economy drives that forced it to use stocks of surplus weapons. Cavalry troopers debated many of the same issues heard in the War Department. A major question revolved around whether the Army should equip its cavalry with repeating rifles or not. The War Department had included issues regarding the cavalry's carbine and revolver in the same small-arms boards used to determine the best infantry weapons. Congress' and the Department's desire for standardization and cost savings drove officers to experiment with various firearms.

After the Civil War, cavalry units operated with two radically different carbines. The Army equipped several regiments, as well as the infantry, with the Spencer repeating carbine. This Civil War veteran was popular among soldiers because of its ability to produce a high rate of fire. The Spencer's relatively short range, 200 yards, would operate well in the forests or woods of Virginia. However, fighting on the Plains required a longer-range weapon; it also did not use the same ammunition as the infantry's Springfield rifle.

Some cavalrymen used a single-shot Sharps .52-cal. breech-loading percussion carbine. In late-1867, the Army had ordered the Sharps Arms Company to modify its carbines to accept a .50/70 cartridge. The Army wanted 31,098 Sharps carbines converted and would then replace the popular Spencer with these.

The 1869 Schofield Board also examined and field-tested a Springfield carbine version, and it became a leading contender in the competition. Like its

Fort Leavenworth, Kansas, served as headquarters of the Department of the Missouri for many years. This photograph of the post was taken in 1890. (RG126 W.C. Brown .189)

Fort Abraham Lincoln in the Dakota Territory was the launching point for 7th Cavalry's ill-fated 1876 Little Big Horn campaign. (RG485 E.S. Godfrey .359)

rifle version, the carbine was a rugged weapon capable of reliable service. The Army settled the ammunition problem. Both the Springfield rifle and carbine accepted a new standard .45-cal. round. The Model 1873 Springfield carbine became the accepted cavalry long-range weapon until the end of the Plains Indian Wars.

Just after the Civil War, the standard Army revolvers were the cap and ball Model 1860 Colt and 1858 New Model Remington Arms Company pistols. These weapons used a cartridge that a soldier had to charge using a front-loading lever and each round was primed with a percussion cap. Both revolvers had six rounds, but the firing and reloading the weapons was extremely slow. Because of these shortcomings, the saber retained its value for close-in, mounted combat.

The Army's focus during the period was clearly on developing a rifle, carbine and revolver that accepted a metallic cartridge. A legal matter held up the use of metallic cartridges though. Smith and Wesson held a patent for rear-loading cartridges for pistols and would have been glad to accept an Army contract. Unfortunately, the service wanted field trials to compare several weapons. Smith and Wesson relented and allowed Remington to experiment applying its patent.

In 1870, the Army formed an Ordnance Board to evaluate pistols. It surprisingly selected a single-shot Remington .50-cal. pistol for limited issue that could only hit a target at 100 yards. Cavalrymen would have to rely on a single-shot weapon and their saber for mounted attacks. The Army also purchased 1,000 six-shot Smith and Wesson .44-cal. (the bore size was actually .45-cal.) pistols. Fortunately for Colt, the Smith and Wesson patent on rear-loading cylinders had expired. Colt sought to build its own rival pistol, and redesigned their older Model 1860 to accept metallic cartridges, with the elimination of the loading lever and the addition of an ejector. Originally, Colt designed their six-shooter as a .44-cal. revolver, but at the insistence of the Ordnance Department modified it to a .45-cal. weapon.

In 1873, after the field trials, the Secretary of War authorized the Ordnance Department to purchase 8,000 of the Model 1873 Colt. The Model 1873 was extremely successful and military and civilian alike knew it as the Peacemaker. Colt sold 13,000 pistols to the Army from 1873 to 1874, and it became the standard service revolver throughout the Army: by 1891 it had bought some 37,000. The Ordnance Department also issued Model 1875 Remington .44-cal. and some Smith and Wesson .45-cal. weapons.

Although cavalrymen rarely employed the saber in combat, many officers believed the shock of using "cold steel" could paralyze an enemy. The saber

took up space and added weight, and, at times, was a nuisance. On campaign, commanders usually told their subordinates to leave the saber at the post. Dismounted cavalrymen could dispatch Indian braves with their Springfield carbines or Colt Peacekeeper at a safer distance than during a saber charge. During the summer of 1876 Sioux campaign, cavalry units went on expedition without their sabers. Saber advocates expressed the opinion that if Custer had taken sabers, he could have provided a better account for his command.

The saber defined the cavalry, and Army regulations continued to authorize its use well into the 20th century and after the elimination of the horse cavalry. Light artillery soldiers could also carry cavalry sabers. Other personnel such as infantry non-commissioned and commissioned officers used swords for parades, and musicians were allowed to carry a shortened sword.

Artillery weapons

Artillery units were not immune to Congress's drive to secure cost savings. The Army used three different types of artillery weapon: cannon, howitzer, and the Gatling gun. Army commanders had seen the devastation wrought by smoothbore cannon against massed formations of infantry. Experienced frontier officers had seen cannons and howitzers in action against Indians before the war too. The Gatling gun was a relatively new invention that was the forerunner of the modern machinegun. Although the Army employed many surplus Civil War-vintage weapons, it did introduce newer weapons such as 3.2in. breech-loading, rifled steel cannon towards the end of the Plains Indian Wars.

Army light artillery companies in the West used two main Civil War-era cannons. In 1856, the Army adopted the 12-pound, smoothbore Napoleon field gun. This piece could fire canister shot or a case shot that was lethal against massed formations. The other popular artillery piece was the 3in. Ordnance rifle (also known as the Rodman gun). The Rodman gun did not require workers to bore out the tube for the rifling. Metalworkers had to cast earlier artillery weapons into one solid piece and then bore out the center, which made many of the artillery pieces structurally weak. However, the manufacturers developed a technique to cast the barrel with molten iron. The Rodman gun's tube lasted longer than a bored-out tube and afforded greater safety for its crew from internal explosions. It had a distinct advantage over the Napoleon, since it used rifling, which improved accuracy.

Artillery location, 1872

	3in. Rifled	12-pdr Bronze	12-pdr Mtn Hwtzr	6-pdr Iron & Bronze	1in. Gatling Gun	0.5-in. Gatling Gun
Depatment of the Missouri						
Fort Bayard			4			
Cheyenne and Arapahoe Agencies						2
Fort Craig		2	3			
Fort Dodge			3			
Fort Garland			2			
Fort Hays			5	1		1
Fort Larned			1			
Fort Leavenworth				5	3	
Fort Lyon		2				
Fort Reno						2
Fort Riley		2				2
Fort Selden		1		1		
Fort Sill	2	2	4			1
Camp Supply	2		5			
Fort Wallace			5			
Fort Wingate				2		
Total	**4**	**9**	**32**	**9**	**3**	**8**

European armies had already started to experiment with and deploy breech-loading steel cannon in their armies. Unfortunately, the US Army had a limited budget that only allowed the Ordnance Department to test a few light artillery pieces. The bulk of the Ordnance Department's funding was devoted to more expensive seacoast heavy artillery that was ill suited to the Plains. The Army eventually began to replace the Napoleon and Rodman guns in 1885, but was not able to replace all pieces until 1892. Several 3.2in. breech-loading guns were taken on campaign in the late-1880s. Artillery officers complained that infantrymen had received breech-loading rifles at the end of the Civil War, while artillery companies operated Civil War relics.

The Army did introduce a Hotchkiss gun. This light piece was a 2-pound, 1.65in. highly mobile howitzer. Infantry and cavalry units could take this weapon on campaign, but the Army employed it late in the Plains Indian Wars period. In December 1890 at Wounded Knee in present day South Dakota, soldiers from the 7th Cavalry and gunners from the 1st Artillery Company E, sought escaping Miniconju tribe members from the Pine Ridge Agency. After a struggle during the disarmament of the braves, fighting broke out between cavalry and Indian warriors. Artillerymen trained their four Hotchkiss guns and devastated the braves.

The Gatling gun was a ten-barreled, hand-cranked gun that used 40-round magazines. A crew could fire up to 350 rounds per minute, assuming the black powder residue did not foul the barrels or they did not jam from overheating. The Army originally accepted it as a flank-defense weapon for all branches of service, especially for infantry. The Ordnance Department requested 209 Gatling guns as auxiliary pieces to the howitzers and cannon in fortifications, but Army field units used it on campaign. The Army did purchase 56 short-barreled Gatling or "camel guns," transported on a cavalry cart. Although the Army classified the Gatling gun as artillery, it did not develop a tactical doctrine for the use of this new rapid-fire weapon.

	3in. Rifled	12-pdr Bronze	12-pdr Mtn Hwtzr	6-pdr Iron & Bronze	1in. Gatling Gun	0.5-in. Gatling Gun
Department of the Platte						
Fort Bridger			2			
Camp Douglas	2	4	3	4	1	
Fort Fetterman		1	6			1
Fort Fred Steele			1			
Fort Laramie	1	4	1			1
Fort McPherson						1
Post of North Platte			1			
Omaha Barracks			4			
Camp Robinson			1		1	1
Fort Sanders			4			
Camp Sheridan						1
Sidney Barracks			1		1	
Camp Stambaugh			1		1	
Total	*3*	*9*	*25*	*4*	*4*	*5*
Department of Dakota						
Fort Abercrombie				2		
Fort Abraham Lincoln	1	1	1		1	1
Fort Benton		2	1			
Fort Buford	1	2		2		
Fort Ellis		2			1	
Lower Brule Agency			5			
Fort Pembina	2	1				
Fort Randall		2	2	1	1	
Fort Rice					1	1
Fort Ripley			1	4		
Fort Seward			2			1
Fort Shaw		2	1			1
Fort Snelling				2		
Standing Rock Agency	2		2			2
Fort Stevenson		3			1	
Fort Sully		2				
Fort Totten	2	2				
Fort Wadsworth			4	1		
Total	*8*	*19*	*19*	*12*	*5*	*6*
GRAND TOTAL	*15*	*37*	*76*	*25*	*12*	*19*

Command, control, communications, and intelligence

The types of issues that affected the outcome of small-unit activities during the Plains Indian Wars included civil-military relations; the vast geographical separation between departmental, regimental, and company commanders; inadequate communications; and patchy information about Indian tribal intentions and movements. Such factors created a very difficult environment for commanders to operate in, and as a result they granted their subordinates greater operational flexibility. For example, on a major campaign, company or battalion commanders received general guidance and direction from their regimental commander, but the companies frequently operated out of sight and communication of their superiors, forcing Army officers to rely on intelligence data. Despite planning and coordination, company or battalion leadership had to make split-second decisions to attack, defend, or retreat—decisions that may or may not have reflected a commander's intent.

Command and control

Regimental commanders normally did not supervise the daily activities of their junior officers. Departmental commanders, instead, had a greater appreciation of the theater and War Department objectives. Post commanders would take command of units residing on their installation. Commanders also took direction from the Bureau of Indian Affairs to retrieve, guard, attack, or arrest Indian tribes who had left the reservation. The command relationships within Army units did not appear distinct or clear, and instead, a junior officer faced many command challenges throughout his tour on the Plains.

The chain of command for the United States Army was as follows. The President of the United States, as commander-in-chief of the armed forces, vested supervision and control of all Army activities with the Secretary of War. Conversely, the Commanding General of the Army, by the late-1870s, had command of the entire Army, line and staff. Before this distinction, as noted previously, secretaries of war could send orders to the field. The Office of the Secretary of War was later restricted to issues involving accountability and administration that were not directly involved in military operations. Support staff and bureaus fell under the direction of the Secretary of War, but these same organizations also answered to the Commanding General of the Army regarding command issues.

Active campaigning seasoned Army officers. Col. E.A. Carr, commander of the 6th US Cavalry (shown here, the first on the left of the three sitting on stools), prepared his officers for conflict with the Sioux at the Pine Ridge Indian Agency, South Dakota in 1890. (RG315 Daughters of the US Army .381)

The Commanding General of the Army relied on his divisional, geographically based commanders to conduct operations. These divisional commanders could command subordinate units, but they usually provided general supervision and control over their departments. A division commander could originate, direct, or approve military operations within his departments. Beyond this, command relationships became blurred. Depending on the type of operation and force composition, several different branches might become involved in an action. Unless designated by higher authority, seniority and rank ruled. For example, a relatively small detachment or three infantry companies might have a colonel as its commander. This unit may have taken the field with a larger cavalry regiment led by a more junior officer, but command fell to the smaller command's officer.

Divisional and departmental commanders also faced another problem. Frequently, these officers did not know the exact location of their subordinates or particular field conditions. Army commanders normally issued overall guidance to their subordinates since the lack of specific information made detailed field orders impractical. Terry, in the Little Big Horn campaign, did not write detailed orders to Custer. Instead, he allowed Custer wide-ranging flexibility to take action. Sheridan also issued general guidance that allowed subordinates to interpret his orders as they saw fit. Top Army commanders might not know what was happening in their commands.

Emory Upton's writings greatly influenced the Army and how it organized its command. Extended formations made commanders frequently lose direct observation of and coordination with their subordinates. Upton believed improved control of forces with modern weapons made massed formations difficult to defend against. These writings encouraged initiative and the concept of providing general guidance.

Fortunately, officers and men throughout the chain of command held positions for long periods. Slow promotions, company and regimental loyalty, and extended postings together did allow officers and enlisted men to understand each other. This allowed the officer to identify leaders among his subordinates and, conversely, the enlisted men could learn the strengths and weaknesses of their officers. However, this situation was a blessing and a curse. Officers and men who trained together for years knew each other's capabilities and trusted each other in battle. Conversely, poor officers could burden a particular command for years.

Officers with brevet ranks granted during Civil War service also presented difficulties to determining proper command. Many officers held temporary or brevet ranks that states had awarded them for their service in volunteer or militia units. Although the Army did not officially recognize these ranks, many officers continued to use these honorific titles. Many officers preferred these brevet ranks to their actual Regular Army ranks, which they held at a much lower grade. Junior officers that may have had one or two brevet ranks could outrank their commanders. Although Congress attempted to stop this practice, vestiges of the system remained.

The supremacy of civil authority over the military also permeated the Plains Indian Wars. The President was the epitome of civilian control and he could direct military activities or change overall Indian policies, but other authorities also prevailed. Army commanders had to respond to a host of governmental and civil authorities. The secretaries of War, Interior, and State had a direct impact on military operations. The Secretary of State's authority allowed him to request that the Army take certain actions in, or to restrict the access to, a Bureau of Indian Affairs reservation or agency. The Secretary of War and the Commanding General of the Army frequently met resistance to their policies from the Interior Department. The Secretary also had some influence over the conduct of Army operations. Commanders who wanted to conduct operations near the Mexican or Canadian borders needed to carefully follow international agreements on pursuing or capturing Indians near the borders.

Army officials and commanders also dealt with Congress as a whole and with individual members who represented local constituent demands. Individual congressmen, as today, had influence over governmental operations through fiscal and legal tools. A local congressman might petition the Secretary of War to establish a post or lend support for added law enforcement to a civilian community.

Several organizations had jurisdictional and legal influence over Army operations on the Plains. Unlike a clearly defined chain of command during a

Philip H. Sheridan served as commander of the Department of the Missouri, Division of the Missouri, and was Commanding General of the Army. He was largely responsible for the conduct of the Plains Indian Wars, and introduced the concept of converging columns to the Department of the Missouri. This photograph was taken in 1884. (RG 262S Indian Wars Collection .94)

Gen. John Schofield served as Commanding General of the Army after Sheridan. He oversaw the successful conclusion of the Plains Indian Wars. (RG113 M.F. Steele .263)

relatively short campaign, Army field commanders had to consider direction and guidance from sources outside of the War Department and difficulties within the uniformed Army. These concerns certainly caused confusion among military personnel and civilians alike.

Communications

The vast network of Western posts forced Army commanders to establish a reasonably fast, reliable communications system in order to fight campaigns or administer everyday military duties. As the frontier's boundaries were pushed to the Pacific, civilian communities also demanded timely communications from the East, wanting commercial, financial, national, and personal news from around the nation. The military and civilian communities used several common communications systems to meet their requirements.

In the field, the Army also developed a set of tactical communications procedures (and equipment) to deal with the Indians. Unfortunately, the state of field communications had not changed significantly since the Civil War. The Army's Signal Corps, responsible for communication devices, felt the sting of Congress's budget cuts. Fortunately, the Secretary of War, despite cuts in manpower, could detail up to 6 officers and 500 enlisted personnel to the Signal Corps from other branches to man its headquarters and field organizations. The duties of the Chief Signal Officer and the Signal Corps ranged from weather reporting to fielding operating communications equipment. These few soldiers deployed, operated, and maintained several communications, including the telegraph, signal flags, torches, and a new device, the heliograph.

The Army did not have a practical field telephone until late-1892 although it experimented with an early version in 1877. Instead, its Signal Corps fell back on a device first used in the Civil War—the telegraph. The Signal Corps was responsible for developing, constructing, and equipping field telegraphs for the military. Field units relied on "United States telegraph lines" (government-owned systems), but could also use commercial systems. The Corps maintained 5,077 miles of telegraph lines at its height in 1881. All official and military telegraphs on a government system had precedence, and Army regulations required telegraph operators to consider them confidential. However, as the railroad and development spread west, commercial telegraph services greatly expanded throughout the frontier. Commercial systems offered their own challenges. Although the telegraph provided commanders with the swiftest form of communication, Army regulations warned officers that it "should be used only in cases where the delay of the mail would be prejudicial to the public interest." Army policy warned officers to avoid "superfluous words not important to the sense of the communications." These limits inhibited detailed command instructions and potential responses. The Army wanted its commanders to use mail since the military could send official business messages postage free.

Unfortunately, even if an Army officer could use the telegraph, the system had many problems with transmission and receipt of messages. Storms, poor equipment, or cut lines might cause the telegraph to fail. The Army established its own telegraph key that used a general service code, but by 1886 had adopted the internationally accepted English Morse code. The War and Navy departments also created a cipher system to transmit coded messages. Each post, if appropriate, had one officer and three enlisted men trained who operated and maintained a telegraph system. The Signal Corps also made assigned personnel report weather details three times a day on the telegraph. By 1880, the Army had established 110 weather stations—an added reason for the Army to increase its telegraph system.

The Signal Corps also had other methods of communication, which included visual devices such as signal flags, torches, and the heliograph. The

Army had used signal flags for years. Signal officers could select from seven different flags that varied in color and size. Moving the flag right indicated a "1" while shifting it left was a "2." A combination of 1s and 2s indicated a specific letter or meaning that made up the general service code mentioned above. Signal flag operators converted to Morse code too. Smoke, environmental conditions, and distance could affect the interpretation of messages. A signal officer used a pair of binoculars to read flag movements at four miles or less, and a telescope for greater distances. Signal Corps officers claimed that observers could decipher messages at 25 miles. One problem that Army officers faced was the possibility of an individual, including Indians, observing the message. Although an enemy might not understand a message, they might interpret heavy communications traffic as a sign of an operation in progress. Another concern for officers was that an observer could not receive a signal flag message during the night or in poor daylight.

Army officers communicated by means of a number of devices. Signal flags were highly effective, but could be interfered with by vegetation, terrain features, or poor visibility. This signal contingent is operating from Fort Reno, Oklahoma Territory, in 1885. (RG315 Daughters of the US Army .252)

Signal officers also employed signal torches for messages. These devices consisted of a copper cylinder filled with combustible fluids (for example, turpentine) and lit with a 6in. cotton wick. The torch's effective range was about ten miles. Other lit devices, such as lanterns, candle-bombs (which exploded at a specified height), and rockets were used too.

The heliograph was an apparatus that used reflected sunlight from a mirror: the Signal Corps adopted it in 1888. Army field units actively used the device in the southwest where strong sunlight and dry weather was the norm. However, some units in the Plains did use the heliograph. One Signal Corps experiment transmitted a heliograph message from Utah to Colorado—some 183 miles.

Intelligence

The Army employed a series of intelligence-gathering methods, a prime requirement for military operations on the Plains. Commanders had few resources to squander against a highly agile foe over thousands of unexplored square miles. Army operations needed current information about tribal movements or intentions. Intelligence-gathering activities included reconnaissance patrols, reports from Indian agents, and the use of Indian and civilian guides and scouts. Army tactics called for advance guards to reconnoiter ahead of any column of soldiers to gather information about the enemy. Bureau of Indian Affairs agents administered reservation activities and could provide a source of intelligence on tribal movements.

Army regulations provided guidance for officers when conducting reconnaissance missions on the battlefield and during combat preparation. If an enemy was present, Army officers conducted daily intelligence gathering missions to observe the terrain, enemy activity, and any signs of attack planning or action. Normally, cavalry patrols conducted these operations in open terrain and infantry soldiers did the same in mountainous areas.

These reconnaissance parties took several precautions, including many that had not changed since the Civil War. They had to leave small detachments of men at intervals to transmit intelligence to the main body of troops as reports filtered back from the advance patrols. Additionally, commanders ordered their men to avoid a fight and to try to avoid detection by the enemy. Finally, upon entering a defile or narrow pass, scouts entered in tandem, not side by side, to avoid the capture of all scouts simultaneously. If the enemy captured or killed the first scout, then the second could escape with any relevant information to the appropriate command.

Regulations cautioned commanders not to enter a defile, woods, village, or other enclosure without suitable reconnaissance. If the commander had planned

Army officers on the Plains had to prepare for and operate in all conditions. These officers wear a number of regulation and non-regulation items of clothing. (RG126 W.C. Brown .83)

to take the offensive, then he could order a reconnaissance or scouting mission to determine the enemy's position, movements, and overall strength. On a major campaign, only the column's commanding general could order his forces to conduct a reconnaissance. Once completed, the reconnaissance officer-in-charge produced reports including a field sketch of the local terrain, enemy strength, and any force dispositions.

Reconnaissance information was not limited to tactical actions only. Each divisional and departmental headquarters used reconnaissance field reports and specific surveys to maintain detailed maps for operational and administrative purposes, prepared by Corps of Engineers officers at these headquarters. Topographical assistants helped these officers perform map-making services.

Indian agents and Army officers frequently disagreed over policy and treatment of tribal members on a reservation. Army officers frequently complained about the poor, corrupt, and ineffective treatment of Indians by these agents that would result in the Army having to resolve problems, sometimes with force. However, as Indians became more dependent on the United States government for food and aid, Indian agents could better observe their numbers, location, and note any tribal discord. Many Indian agents sought to "civilize" their Indian charges through Christian principles and aid, which did not include any dealings with the Army. They resisted any attempts by the Army to take over the administration of reservations and agencies because of the belief that harsh military action was counterproductive to their efforts to pacify the tribes. Many Indian agents refused to cooperate with Army requests for information on the locations of tribes or individuals.

The Army used Indian and civilian guides and scouts in a number of campaigns. During the Little Big Horn campaign, Indian scouts provided a major source of information about the location of the main Sioux camp. These guides and scouts offered a command the ability to communicate with Indians, use their geographic knowledge, and interpret physical evidence such as tracking movements. An Arikara-Sioux guide, Bloody Knife, had worked for the Army since 1868 and accompanied Custer to his death in 1876. Civilian guides and interpreters also supplied the Army with knowledge gleaned from years of experience living with Indians or making a living on the Plains, like buffalo hunting. Indian scouts could also serve in an enlisted status, receiving regular pay and rations, and a bonus of 100 dollars if they successfully located a specific target such as an Indian village.

Unit status

The Army assigned numerous regiments to the Division of the Missouri, some of which served long and distinguished tours of duty, such as the 7th Cavalry Regiment. Not all regiments were deployed on the frontier for long periods, as units were transferred to other areas after only a few years. The Army rotated some units simply because of poor living conditions, which it did not wish to burden one particular regiment with. The Army also had to contend with frontier emergencies, with regiments rushed into an area in response to a crisis. Almost every existing Army regiment had units that served on the Plains. Some regiments provided years of duty for the Military Division of the Missouri, while others had only a company, battery, or troop in service. Each of these regiments has a unique history and story.

Despite the move onto agency land, most tribes did not lose their cultural identity. These Sioux tribe members are performing a native dance at the Rosebud Agency, Dakota Territory, in 1884. (RG315 Daughters of the US Army .456)

Infantry

1st Infantry

The regiment was formed as the 2nd Infantry on March 3, 1791 in New England. The unit absorbed several regiments after the War of 1812 when it was reconstituted as the 1st Infantry. In April 1869, the 1st and the 43rd Infantry, Veteran Reserve Corps merged. The regiment fought the Sioux during the Pine Ridge campaign, which included the Battle of Wounded Knee. The regiment served throughout the Dakotas and Montana from 1874 to about 1879.

2nd Infantry

This Regular Army regiment was formed originally as the 6th Infantry on April 12, 1808. From April to October 1815, the Army combined the 6th with the 22nd, 23rd, and 32nd Infantry to form the 2nd Infantry. Congressional budget reductions in 1869 forced the Army to combine the 16th Infantry and the 2nd at Atlanta, Georgia. The unit campaigned during the Pine Ridge campaign from 1890 to 1891.

3rd Infantry

The 3rd Infantry Regiment could trace its direct descent from the First American Regiment that was organized in the summer of 1784. The unit was redesignated as the 1st Infantry on March 3, 1791. Between May and October 1815, the regiment combined with the 5th, 17th, 19th, and 28th infantry regiments to form the 3rd Infantry. After the Civil War, the Army merged the 3rd Infantry and half of the 37th Infantry. The unit's major campaign participation was in Kansas in 1868 and Montana during 1887. The regiment also contributed soldiers to the Pine Ridge campaign.

4th Infantry

The 4th Infantry had its roots in the 14th Infantry. The army created the 14th on January 11, 1812. After the War of 1812, the army reorganized the 4th when it merged it with the 18th, 20th, 36th, and 38th infantry regiments. In March 1869, the 4th absorbed the 30th Infantry. The regiment participated in the Little Big Horn campaign and served extensively in Kansas during the 1860s against the Comanche, Kiowa, Cheyenne, and Arapahoe nations.

Infantry companies typically fielded 30-40 men. This 1886 infantry encampment shown belongs to Company B, 3rd US Infantry, commanded by Capt. John P. Thompson. (RG315 Daughters of the US Army .390)

5th Infantry

The 5th Infantry Regiment was formed on April 12, 1808. The unit was first constituted as the 4th Infantry, but after it was consolidated with the 9th, 13th, 21st, and 40th infantry regiments, it became the 5th Infantry in October 1815. In June 1869, the army consolidated the 5th with half of the 37th Infantry Regiment. The 5th Infantry earned recognition from the War Department for its actions during the Little Big Horn campaign and service in Montana in 1879, 1880, 1881, and 1887.

6th Infantry

The army constituted the 6th on January 11, 1812 as the 11th Infantry. After the War of 1812, the unit merged with the 25th, 27th, 29th, and 37th to become the 6th. On May 1, 1869 the army combined the regiment with the 42nd Infantry, Veteran Reserve Corps. The 6th Infantry Regiment participated in campaigns against the Cheyenne, at Little Big Horn, in activities in North Dakota during 1872 and 1873, and in the 1879 Montana actions.

7th Infantry

The 7th Infantry was created on January 11, 1812 as the 8th Infantry. Between May and October 1815, the Army forced the 8th to combine with the 24th and 29th to form the new 7th Infantry. From May to June 1869, the 7th acquired personnel from the 36th Infantry. The 7th's officers and men participated at Little Big Horn, Pine Ridge, actions in Wyoming during 1866, and the 1872 Montana activities.

8th Infantry

The Army formed the 8th Infantry on July 5, 1838. The Army merged the 8th with the 33rd Infantry in May 1869. The unit served in campaigns in Montana during 1872 and patrolled several reservations to ensure Sioux and Miniconju did not abscond from their agencies.

9th Infantry

The 9th Infantry formed at Fort Monroe, Virginia, on March 26, 1855. After the Civil War, the Army forced the 27th Infantry to join with the 9th. The 9th Infantry served in the Little Big Horn campaign and the activities in Wyoming during 1866 and 1867. The Army posted the regiment to Sioux reservations in Nebraska and Wyoming from 1874 to 1876.

10th Infantry

The Army authorized the creation of the 10th Infantry on March 3, 1855. Throughout April 1855, the 10th organized itself at Carlisle Barracks, Pennsylvania. The economy moves of Congress after the Civil War forced the 10th to combine with the 26th Infantry between June and July 1869. In June 1884, the Army assigned the regiment to the Department of the Missouri. In one instance, on March 16, 1885, a detachment of soldiers rescued civil authorities in Colfax County, New Mexico, from outlaws who had laid siege to county offices.

11th Infantry

Civil War demands forced the War Department to create the 11th Infantry on May 2, 1861 as the 2nd Battalion, 15th Infantry. The unit organized on May 6, 1862 at Newport Barracks, Kentucky, as the 24th Infantry. Post-Civil War consolidations with the 29th Infantry increased the 11th. The 11th fought against the Comanche, Cheyenne, and Kiowa tribes.

12th Infantry

Congress authorized the creation of the unit as the 1st Battalion, 12th Infantry on May 3, 1861. The unit formed at Fort Hamilton, New York, on October 20, 1861. The Army reorganized and realigned it as the 12th Infantry Regiment on December 7, 1866. The Army stationed the regiment in Kansas in 1865; it saw action during the Pine Ridge campaign.

13th Infantry

The Army created the 13th as the 1st Battalion, 13th Infantry between July 27, 1861 and April 1, 1862 at Jefferson Barracks, Missouri, and Alton, Illinois. The Army later expanded the unit to become the 13th Infantry Regiment on September 21, 1866. The regiment conducted extensive military operations in North Dakota during 1866 and in Montana two years later. The regiment also deployed companies throughout the Department of the Platte during the late 1860s and through to 1872.

14th Infantry

Abraham Lincoln's May 1861 Army expansion allowed the War Department to raise the 2nd Battalion, 14th Infantry; it later expanded into the 14th Infantry Regiment on September 21, 1866. The 1869 Army reorganization forced it to combine with the 45th Infantry, Veteran Reserve Corps. The Army posted the regiment throughout the Department of Dakota and the Platte. After Little Big Horn, the 14th supported efforts to track down renegade Sioux braves. Over a three-month period, they marched 1,139 miles.

15th Infantry

The Army's Civil War expansion created the 15th Infantry, originally as the 1st Battalion, 15th Infantry. The regiment formed at Newport Barracks, Kentucky, from September to October 1861. After the war, the Army designated the unit the 15th Infantry. On August 12, 1869 the 15th absorbed the 35th Infantry. The regiment served in the Department of Dakota from October 1882 to May 1890.

16th Infantry

The 16th Infantry has its roots in the May 1861 Army expansion that formed the 1st Battalion, 11th Infantry. Congress allowed the Army to expand the unit into the 11th Regiment on December 5, 1866 and it consolidated the 11th with the 34th Infantry to become the 16th Infantry in 1869. The regiment's main experience of fighting the Indians was during the Pine Ridge campaign.

Winter campaigning proved an arduous task. These soldiers from Company C, 17th Infantry, participated in the Pine Ridge campaign in January 1891. (RG315 Daughters of the US Army .401)

17th Infantry

In the midst of the Civil War expansion, the 17th Infantry formed on July 6, 1861 as the 1st Battalion, 15th Infantry. The Army later reorganized the battalion as the 15th Infantry Regiment on December 13, 1866. Three years later, on June 1, 1869 the 15th combined with the 44th Infantry from the Veteran Reserve Corps. The regiment operated in the Department of Dakota from 1870 for 16 years and the Army later transferred it to the Department of the Platte until the end of the Plains Indian Wars. The regiment actively campaigned during the Little Big Horn and the Pine Ridge campaigns.

18th Infantry

The Army created the 18th's founder unit at Camp Thomas, Ohio on July 22, 1861; it became a full regiment on December 31, 1866. The 18th expanded when the 25th Infantry's personnel joined the regiment on April 28, 1869. The Army sent the regiment to the Department of the Missouri after the Civil War and it later served in the Department of the Platte.

19th Infantry

The Army formed the 1st Battalion, 19th Infantry at Indianapolis, Indiana, on July 9, 1861. The organization expanded until it consisted of three battalions and it became a full regiment on October 1, 1866. The 28th Infantry's personnel joined the 15th as part of a general consolidation on March 15, 1869. The Army assigned the unit to the Department of the Missouri in June 1874 and it served throughout Kansas.

20th Infantry

The Army organized the 2nd Battalion, 11th Infantry on June 6, 1862 at Fort Independence, Massachusetts. The unit became the 20th Infantry on December 6, 1866. By March 15, 1869 the 20th became part of the Department of Dakota where its companies guarded Indian agencies and railways, and served as escorts. The regiment served during the Little Big Horn and Pine Ridge campaigns.

21st Infantry

On May 20, 1862 at Fort Hamilton, New York, the Army established the 2nd Battalion, 12th Infantry. This battalion reformed as the 21st Infantry on December 7, 1866. The regiment's size increased with the addition of the 32nd Infantry during August 1869. The 21st became part of the Department of the Platte in 1884.

22nd Infantry

The Army's 22nd Infantry was first formed as the 2nd Battalion, 13th Infantry. The unit organized at Camp Dennison, Ohio, on May 15, 1865. On September 21, 1866 the battalion became the 22nd Infantry. Throughout May 1869, the Army reformed the regiment with the 31st Infantry. The 22nd served during the Little Big Horn and Pine Ridge campaigns.

23rd Infantry

The 23rd Infantry's founder unit was the 1st Battalion, 14th Infantry, which the Army organized on July 8, 1861 at Fort Turmbull, Connecticut. The War Department redesignated it the 2nd Battalion, 14th Infantry on April 30, 1862 and as the 23rd Infantry on September 23, 1866. The regiment participated in the Little Big Horn campaign.

24th Infantry

The Army's 24th Infantry descended from two African-American infantry regiments, the 38th and 41st Infantry. The two regiments came into being on July 28, 1866 and merged in 1869. The Army assigned the

24th to the Department of the Missouri in the early 1880s, but it did not go on campaign.

25th Infantry

Like the 24th Infantry, the 25th Infantry was an African-American regiment whose origins lay in a post-Civil War reorganization of July 28, 1866. The Army formed the 39th and 40th infantry regiments, which became the 25th Infantry in May 1869. In April 1880, the War Department ordered the regiment to the Department of Dakota with most of the units in South and North Dakota. The 25th Infantry relocated to Montana. The unit served in the Pine Ridge campaign.

Other infantry regiments

The Army deployed several regiments for two to three years to the Plains. The 27th, 30th, 31st, 36th, and 38th infantry regiments served for several years after the Civil War in the Division of the Missouri. All these units were disbanded after 1869.

Infantry regiments: authorized strength, October 14, 1876 (see page 92 for rank abbreviations)

Regiment	Col.	Lt.Col.	Maj.	Capt.	Adj.*	Reg.QM*	1st Lt.	2nd Lt.	Chap.
1st	1	1	1	10	1	1	10	10	0
2nd	1	1	1	10	1	1	10	10	0
3rd	1	1	1	10	1	1	10	10	0
4th	1	1	1	10	1	1	10	10	0
5th	1	1	1	10	1	1	10	10	0
6th	1	1	1	10	1	1	10	10	0
7th	1	1	1	10	1	1	10	10	0
8th	1	1	1	10	1	1	10	10	0
9th	1	1	1	10	1	1	10	10	0
10th	1	1	1	10	1	1	10	10	0
11th	1	1	1	10	1	1	10	10	0
12th	1	1	1	10	1	1	10	10	0
13th	1	1	1	10	1	1	10	10	0
14th	1	1	1	10	1	1	10	10	0
15th	1	1	1	10	1	1	10	10	0
16th	1	1	1	10	1	1	10	10	0
17th	1	1	1	10	1	1	10	10	0
18th	1	1	1	10	1	1	10	10	0
19th	1	1	1	10	1	1	10	10	0
20th	1	1	1	10	1	1	10	10	0
21st	1	1	1	10	1	1	10	10	0
22nd	1	1	1	10	1	1	10	10	0
23rd	1	1	1	10	1	1	10	10	0
24th	1	1	1	10	1	1	10	10	1
25th	1	1	1	10	1	1	10	10	1
Total	**25**	**25**	**25**	**250**	**25**	**25**	**250**	**250**	**2**

Note: * manned by an extra lieutenant.

(continued on page 84)

Regiment	Sgt. Maj.	QM Sgt.	Ch. Mus.	Pr. Mus.	1st Sgt.	Sgt.	Cpl.	Mus.	Artf.	Wag.	Pvt.
1st	1	1	1	2	10	40	40	20	20	10	400
2nd	1	1	1	2	10	40	40	20	20	10	400
3rd	1	1	1	2	10	40	40	20	20	10	400
4th	1	1	1	2	10	40	40	20	20	10	400
5th	1	1	1	2	10	40	40	20	20	10	400
6th	1	1	1	2	10	40	40	20	20	10	400
7th	1	1	1	2	10	40	40	20	20	10	400
8th	1	1	1	2	10	40	40	20	20	10	400
9th	1	1	1	2	10	40	40	20	20	10	400
10th	1	1	1	2	10	40	40	20	20	10	400
11th	1	1	1	2	10	40	40	20	20	10	400
12th	1	1	1	2	10	40	40	20	20	10	160
13th	1	1	1	2	10	40	40	20	20	10	400
14th	1	1	1	2	10	40	40	20	20	10	400
15th	1	1	1	2	10	40	40	20	20	10	260
16th	1	1	1	2	10	40	40	20	20	10	400
17th	1	1	1	2	10	40	40	20	20	10	400
18th	1	1	1	2	10	40	40	20	20	10	400
19th	1	1	1	2	10	40	40	20	20	10	260
20th	1	1	1	2	10	40	40	20	20	10	260
21st	1	1	1	2	10	40	40	20	20	10	160
22nd	1	1	1	2	10	40	40	20	20	10	304
23rd	1	1	1	2	10	40	40	20	20	10	260
24th	1	1	1	2	10	40	40	20	20	10	160
25th	1	1	1	2	10	40	40	20	20	10	160
Total	**25**	**25**	**25**	**50**	**250**	**1,000**	**1,000**	**500**	**500**	**250**	**8,384**

Regiment	Comm. officers	Enlisted	Total
1st	35	545	580
2nd	35	545	580
3rd	35	545	580
4th	35	545	580
5th	35	545	580
6th	35	545	580
7th	35	545	580
8th	35	545	580
9th	35	545	580
10th	35	545	580
11th	35	545	580
12th	35	305	340
13th	35	545	580
14th	35	545	580

 (continued on page 85)

Regiment	Comm. officers	Enlisted	Total
15th	35	405	440
16th	35	545	580
17th	35	545	580
18th	35	545	580
19th	35	405	440
20th	35	405	440
21st	35	305	340
22nd	35	449	484
23rd	35	405	440
24th	36	305	341
25th	36	305	341
Total	**877**	**12,009**	**12,886**

Infantry regiments: actual strength, October 14, 1876

Regiment	Col.	Lt.Col.	Maj.	Capt.	Adj.*	Reg.QM*	1st Lt.	2nd Lt.	Chap.
1st	1	1	1	10	1	1	10	10	0
2nd	1	1	1	10	1	1	10	10	0
3rd	1	1	1	10	1	1	10	10	0
4th	1	1	1	10	1	1	10	10	0
5th	1	1	1	10	1	1	10	10	0
6th	1	1	1	10	1	1	10	10	0
7th	1	1	1	10	1	1	10	10	0
8th	1	1	1	10	1	1	10	10	0
9th	1	1	1	10	1	1	10	10	0
10th	1	1	1	10	1	1	10	10	0
11th	1	1	1	10	1	1	10	9	0
12th	1	1	1	10	1	1	10	10	0
13th	1	1	1	10	1	1	10	10	0
14th	1	1	1	10	1	1	10	10	0
15th	1	1	1	10	1	1	10	10	0
16th	1	1	1	10	1	1	10	10	0
17th	1	1	1	10	1	1	10	8	0
18th	1	1	1	10	1	1	10	10	0
19th	1	1	1	10	1	1	10	10	0
20th	1	1	1	10	1	1	10	10	0
21st	1	1	1	10	1	1	10	10	0
22nd	1	1	1	10	1	1	10	9	0
23rd	1	1	1	10	1	1	10	10	0
24th	1	1	1	10	1	1	10	9	1
25th	1	1	1	10	1	1	10	9	1
Total	**25**	**25**	**25**	**250**	**25**	**25**	**250**	**244**	**2**

Note: * manned by an extra lieutenant.

(continued on page 86)

Regiment	Sgt. Maj.	QM Sgt.	Ch. Mus.	Pr. Mus.	1st Sgt.	Sgt.	Cpl.	Mus.	Artf.	Wag.	Pvt.
1st	1	1	1	2	10	32	32	19	0	3	427
2nd	0	1	1	1	10	38	26	16	2	1	257
3rd	1	1	1	2	10	34	26	13	2	0	355
4th	1	1	1	1	10	39	35	18	3	0	439
5th	1	1	1	2	10	39	33	19	2	0	402
6th	1	1	1	2	10	35	34	15	5	0	382
7th	0	1	1	1	10	36	37	15	3	1	332
8th	1	1	1	2	10	39	34	18	0	0	393
9th	1	1	1	2	10	39	36	20	4	0	465
10th	1	1	1	2	10	38	33	15	12	1	365
11th	1	1	1	2	10	37	37	13	8	0	442
12th	1	1	1	2	10	35	29	15	0	0	258
13th	1	1	1	1	10	33	30	14	1	0	379
14th	1	1	1	2	10	38	35	19	2	0	410
15th	1	1	1	2	10	35	26	17	0	1	406
16th	1	1	1	2	10	35	33	21	5	0	277
17th	1	1	1	2	9	36	40	17	5	0	392
18th	1	1	1	2	10	37	31	16	1	0	274
19th	1	1	1	2	10	37	29	18	3	0	255
20th	1	1	1	2	9	33	34	16	1	0	291
21st	1	1	1	2	10	30	32	18	0	0	276
22nd	1	1	1	2	10	39	35	17	0	0	396
23rd	1	1	1	2	10	39	39	18	2	0	388
24th	1	0	0	2	10	21	19	11	0	0	296
25th	1	1	1	1	9	35	32	11	0	0	326
Total	*23*	*24*	*24*	*45*	*247*	*889*	*807*	*409*	*61*	*7*	*8,883*

Regiment	Comm. officers	Enlisted	Total
1st	35	528	563
2nd	35	353	388
3rd	35	445	480
4th	35	548	583
5th	35	510	545
6th	35	486	521
7th	35	437	472
8th	35	499	534
9th	35	579	614
10th	35	479	514
11th	34	552	586
12th	35	352	387
13th	35	471	506
14th	35	519	554

 (continued on page 87)

Regiment	Comm. officers	Enlisted	Total
15th	35	500	535
16th	35	386	421
17th	33	504	537
18th	35	374	409
19th	35	357	392
20th	35	389	424
21st	35	371	406
22nd	34	502	536
23rd	35	501	536
24th	35	360	395
25th	35	417	452
Total	*871*	*11,419*	*12,290*

Cavalry

1st Cavalry

The War Department formed the United States Regiment of Dragoons on March 4, 1833 at Jefferson Barracks, Missouri. This regiment became the 1st Cavalry on August 3, 1861. The regiment served primarily on the Pacific coast after the Civil War until about 1883 when it became part of the Department of Dakota. The regiment fought several engagements with the Crow and Cheyenne tribes, particularly the former during 1887 in Montana.

2nd Cavalry

The 2nd Cavalry was the direct descendent of the 2nd Regiment of Dragoons that the War Department constituted on May 23, 1836. The regiment evolved into the 2nd Regiment of Riflemen on March 5, 1843. The War Department remounted the unit as the 2nd Cavalry on August 3, 1861. The Army stationed the 2nd on the Plains from 1868 to about 1883. The regiment saw service during the Little Big Horn campaign and throughout Kansas, Wyoming, and Montana.

3rd Cavalry

The Army organized the 3rd's founder unit, the Regiment of Mounted Riflemen, at Jefferson Barracks, Missouri, on October 12, 1846. Shortly after the Civil War began, the unit became the 3rd Cavalry on August 2, 1861. The 3rd spent most of its assignment on the Plains fighting Comanche, Sioux, and Cheyenne braves and saw action in the Little Big Horn campaign.

4th Cavalry

The 4th Cavalry was originally formed and organized as the 1st Cavalry on March 26, 1855 at Jefferson Barracks, Missouri. The unit became the 4th Cavalry on August 3, 1861. It served from about 1875 to 1886 on the Plains, undertaking actions against the Cheyenne and participating in the Little Big Horn campaign.

5th Cavalry

The 5th Cavalry's founder unit was the 2nd Cavalry, which the Army created in Louisville, Kentucky, on May 26, 1855. Civil War exigencies forced the Army to redesignate the 2nd as the 5th Cavalry on August 3, 1861. The regiment had an extensive service record on the Plains: its primary service revolved around campaigns against the Sioux, Cheyenne, and Comanche tribes. The 5th also participated in the Little Big Horn campaign.

6th Cavalry

The 6th was originally organized as the 3rd Cavalry on June 18, 1861 at Pittsburgh, Pennsylvania. It became the 6th Cavalry on August 3, 1861. The 6th served on the Plains from 1871 to 1874 and from 1884 to 1891. Its major action was against the Sioux during the Pine Ridge campaign.

7th Cavalry

The 7th Cavalry was formed on September 21, 1866 at Fort Riley, Kansas. The 7th performed for many years on the Plains, and served throughout the Southern and Northern Plains almost uninterrupted from 1866 to 1891. The regiment was involved in the Little Big Horn and the Pine Ridge campaigns, and its campaign against Sioux braves at the Battle of Wounded Knee effectively ended the Plains Indian wars.

8th Cavalry

The Army created the 8th Cavalry at Angel Island (San Francisco Bay) on September 21, 1866. The unit served intermittently on the Plains and its major campaign activity in the region was at Pine Ridge.

9th Cavalry

The 9th Cavalry was one of two African-American cavalry units, and was formed in October 1866 at Greenville, Louisiana. The Army's formation of the regiment was through the enlistment of volunteers from several volunteer African-American units created during the Civil War. Units from the 9th Cavalry served in the Plains from 1876 to 1891. The 9th operated in the Pine Ridge campaign.

10th Cavalry

The 10th Cavalry Regiment was the second African-American cavalry unit and was formed on September 21, 1866 at Fort Leavenworth, Kansas. The 10th served primarily in the Department of the Missouri from its creation until 1872. The 10th conducted operations against the Cheyenne, Kiowa, and Comanche tribes during the period. The regiment returned to duty on the Plains from 1877 to 1878 when some companies served on the Southern Plains.

Cavalry regiments: authorized strength, October 14, 1876 (see page 92 for rank abbreviations)									
Regiment	Col.	Lt.Col.	Maj.	Capt.	Adj.*	Reg.QM*	1st Lt.	2nd Lt.	Chap.
1st	1	1	3	12	1	1	12	12	0
2nd	1	1	3	12	1	1	12	12	0
3rd	1	1	3	12	1	1	12	12	0
4th	1	1	3	12	1	1	12	12	0
5th	1	1	3	12	1	1	12	12	0
6th	1	1	3	12	1	1	12	12	0
7th	1	1	3	12	1	1	12	12	0
8th	1	1	3	12	1	1	12	12	0
9th	1	1	3	12	1	1	12	12	1
10th	1	1	3	12	1	1	12	12	1
Total	*10*	*10*	*30*	*120*	*10*	*10*	*120*	*120*	*2*

Note: * manned by an extra lieutenant.

Regiment	Sgt. Maj.	QM Sgt.	Ch. Mus.	Sdlr. Sgt.	Ch. Tru.	1st Sgt.	Sgt.	Cpl.	Tru.	Fr./ Bsm.	Sdlr.	Wag.	Pvt.
1st	1	1	1	1	1	12	60	48	24	24	12	12	648
2nd	1	1	1	1	1	12	60	48	24	24	12	12	1,005
3rd	1	1	1	1	1	12	60	48	24	24	12	12	1,005
4th	1	1	1	1	1	12	60	48	24	24	12	12	1,005
5th	1	1	1	1	1	12	60	48	24	24	12	12	1,005
6th	1	1	1	1	1	12	60	48	24	24	12	12	648
7th	1	1	1	1	1	12	60	48	24	24	12	12	1,005
8th	1	1	1	1	1	12	60	48	24	24	12	12	1,005
9th	1	1	1	1	1	12	60	48	24	24	12	12	648
10th	1	1	1	1	1	12	60	48	24	24	12	12	1,005
Total	10	10	10	10	10	120	600	480	240	240	120	120	8,979

Regiment	Comm. officers	Enlisted	Total
1st	43	845	888
2nd	43	1,202	1,245
3rd	43	1,202	1,245
4th	43	1,202	1,245
5th	43	1,202	1,245
6th	43	845	888
7th	43	1,202	1,245
8th	43	1,202	1,245
9th	44	845	889
10th	44	1,202	1,246
Total	432	10,949	11,381

Cavalry regiments: actual strength, October 14, 1876

Regiment	Col.	Lt.Col.	Maj.	Capt.	Adj.*	Reg.QM*	1st Lt.	2nd Lt.	Chap.
1st	1	1	3	12	1	1	12	12	0
2nd	1	1	3	12	1	1	12	12	0
3rd	1	1	3	12	1	1	12	11	0
4th	1	1	3	12	1	1	12	12	0
5th	1	1	3	12	1	1	12	12	0
6th	1	1	3	12	1	1	12	12	0
7th	1	1	3	12	1	1	12	12	0
8th	1	1	3	12	1	1	12	11	0
9th	1	1	3	12	1	1	12	7	1
10th	1	1	3	12	1	1	12	6	1
Total	10	10	30	120	10	10	120	107	2

Note: * manned by an extra lieutenant.

(continued on page 90)

Regiment	Sgt. Maj.	QM Sgt.	Ch. Mus.	Sdlr. Sgt.	Ch. Tru.	1st Sgt.	Sgt.	Cpl.	Tru.	Fr./ Bsm.	Sdlr.	Wag.	Pvt.
1st	1	1	1	1	1	12	56	45	18	23	11	1	603
2nd	1	1	1	0	0	12	60	45	17	22	12	0	771
3rd	1	1	1	1	1	12	57	43	19	22	8	6	716
4th	1	0	0	0	1	12	56	41	22	24	12	12	795
5th	0	1	1	1	1	12	58	45	15	20	12	6	899
6th	1	1	1	1	1	12	53	39	20	19	12	7	570
7th	1	1	1	1	1	12	57	42	20	24	12	3	857
8th	1	1	1	1	1	12	56	42	22	22	12	0	588
9th	1	1	1	0	1	12	46	37	23	22	11	0	493
10th	1	1	1	1	1	12	53	40	21	24	11	3	623
Total	9	9	9	7	9	120	552	419	197	222	113	38	6,915

Regiment	Comm. officers	Enlisted	Total
1st	43	774	817
2nd	43	942	985
3rd	42	888	930
4th	43	976	1,019
5th	43	1,071	1,114
6th	43	737	780
7th	43	1,032	1,075
8th	42	759	801
9th	39	648	687
10th	38	792	830
Total	419	8,619	9,038

The army conducted numerous winter campaigns to catch tribes in their encampments. Here, Capt. John Quincy Adams leads B Troop, 1st Cavalry from Fort Keogh at the start of the Pine Ridge campaign on December 7, 1890. (RG315 Daughters of the US Army .96)

Artillery

1st Artillery

Congress authorized the organization of the 1st, 2nd, 3rd, and 4th artillery regiments under the Act of March 2, 1821. The Army did previously possess artillery, but the units evolved as part of the Legion of the United States, Corps of Artillerists and Engineers, Light Artillery, Corps of Artillery, and finally to the organization seen on the Plains. Although the majority of 1st Artillery's units served as seacoast fortification artillery, some companies, later batteries, served at posts on the Plains. At the Battle of Wounded Knee, Light Battery E supported combat operations—the only Plains campaign participation of 1st Artillery.

2nd Artillery
In 1869, a company from the 1st established a light artillery school at Fort Riley, Kansas. On the Plains, the regiment provided support to Army activities in Kansas after Little Big Horn. The Army sent four companies to the Indian Territories and Fort Dodge.

3rd Artillery
The 3rd Artillery provided very limited services on the Plains. A single company served at Fort McPherson, Nebraska, in 1867.

4th Artillery
Although most of 4th Artillery's operations involved garrison duty at Indian agencies, it did accompany units on campaign, notably during Little Big Horn.

5th Artillery
On January 7, 1861 the Army formed a single company of four artillery pieces at the US Military Academy, West Point, New York: this laid the foundations for the 5th Artillery Regiment. The Civil War expansion soon increased the number of artillery units, a factor which led to the creation of the 5th Artillery. Some of its units served in Nebraska in the Department of the Platte.

Artillery regiments: authorized strength, October 14, 1876 (see page 92 for rank abbreviations)

Regiment	Col.	Lt.Col.	Maj.	Capt.	Adj.*	Reg.QM*	1st Lt.	2nd Lt.
1st	1	1	3	12	1	1	24	13
2nd	1	1	3	12	1	1	24	13
3rd	1	1	3	12	1	1	24	13
4th	1	1	3	12	1	1	24	13
5th	1	1	3	12	1	1	24	13
Total	5	5	15	60	5	5	120	65

Note: * manned by an extra lieutenant.

Regiment	Sgt. Maj.	QM Sgt.	Ch. Mus.	Pr. Mus.	1st Sgt.	Sgt.	Cpl.	Mus.	Artf.	Wag.	Pvt.
1st	1	1	1	2	12	50	48	24	24	12	265
2nd	1	1	1	2	12	50	48	24	24	12	385
3rd	1	1	1	2	12	50	48	24	24	12	265
4th	1	1	1	2	12	50	48	24	24	12	265
5th	1	1	1	2	12	50	48	24	24	12	465
Total	5	5	5	10	60	250	240	120	120	60	1,645

Regiment	Comm. officers	Enlisted	Total
1st	56	440	496
2nd	56	560	616
3rd	56	440	496
4th	56	440	496
5th	56	640	696
Total	280	2,520	2,800

Artillery regiments: actual strength, October 14, 1876

Regiment	Col.	Lt.Col.	Maj.	Capt.	Adj.*	Reg.QM*	1st Lt.	2nd Lt.
1st	1	1	3	12	1	1	24	13
2nd	1	1	3	12	1	1	24	12
3rd	1	1	3	12	1	1	24	13
4th	1	1	3	12	1	1	24	13
5th	1	1	3	12	1	1	24	13
Total	5	5	15	60	5	5	120	64

Note: * manned by an extra lieutenant.

Regiment	Sgt. Maj.	QM Sgt.	Ch. Mus.	Pr. Mus.	1st Sgt.	Sgt.	Cpl.	Mus.	Artf.	Wag.	Pvt.
1st	1	1	1	2	11	47	44	21	8	1	403
2nd	1	1	1	2	12	45	39	21	3	0	437
3rd	1	1	1	2	12	47	37	21	7	1	408
4th	1	1	1	2	12	43	36	22	3	0	402
5th	0	1	1	2	11	39	27	17	4	0	350
Total	4	5	5	10	58	221	183	102	25	2	2,000

Regiment	Comm. officers	Enlisted	Total
1st	56	540	596
2nd	55	562	617
3rd	56	538	594
4th	56	523	579
5th	56	452	508
Total	279	2,615	2,894

Key to rank abbreviations:

Adj.	Adjutant	Lt.Col.	Lieutenant-Colonel	Sgt.	Sergeant
Artf.	Artificer	Maj.	Major	Sgt.Maj.	Sergeant-Major
Capt.	Captain	Mus.	Musician	Tru.	Trumpeter
Chap.	Chaplain	Pvt.	Private	Wag.	Wagoneer
Ch.Mus.	Chief Musician	Pr.Mus.	Principal Musician	1st Sgt.	First Sergeant
Ch.Tru.	Chief Trumpeter	QM Sgt.	Quartermaster Sergeant	1st Lt.	First-Lieutenant
Col.	Colonel	Reg.QM	Regimental Quartermaster	2nd Lt.	Second-Lieutenant
Cpl.	Corporal	Sdlr.	Saddler		
Fr./Bsm.	Farriers and blacksmiths	Sdlr. Sgt.	Saddler Sergeant		

Lessons learned

The Plains Indian Wars were a challenge for the United States Army after the Civil War. The military's leaders, faced with a new type of conflict, had to adjust strategies and tactics for an enemy that the Army was ill equipped, ill trained, and poorly prepared to fight. Officers and enlisted men had to use antiquated weapons, face difficult terrain spread across the continent, and fight a determined adversary, with limited resources. Despite these difficulties, the Army was able to support the westward expansion of the United States.

The conflict provided an opportunity for change within the Army. Emory Upton's fresh emphasis on individual initiative and leader development encouraged Army officers to observe and seek out opportunities. The Plains Indian Wars allowed many junior and senior officers to apply these ideas in the field.

The Wars tested the mettle of both officers and their men, even though the prolonged conflict was not as costly as the Civil War. They faced an enemy that was more flexible, had better knowledge of the terrain, had more modern weapons, and was more mobile. The Army's leaders also had to divide their time between fighting hostile tribes and protecting emigrants, construction projects, and survey teams, as well as acting as the only law enforcement body for civilian and Indian populations. Such responsibilities did allow Army officers an insight into a host of civilian liaison issues though, valuable lessons that would aid them in later conflicts and with the expansion of America's overseas territories in the late-19th century. The actions fought on the Plains provided valuable experience for the officers and men who would serve the American military in the ensuing years and decades. Many of the regiments that served on the Plains went to war in Cuba and the Philippines in 1898 during the Spanish–American War, the first major overseas effort of the United States military. The lessons learned would also help shape Army reforms instigated both before and during World War I.

The demise of the Plains Indians was partly a result of extensive buffalo hunting by white hunters. The buffalo was a source of food, clothing, and other materials, as well as being of religious and cultural significance. (RG95 Fort Sill Collection)

These Indian warriors fought the Army in the Pine Ridge campaign of 1890, the last organized opposition to the United States government. (RG485 E.S. Godfrey .340)

Bibliography

Burnside, Ambrose *Reorganization of the Army* (Washington, DC: United States Senate 45th Congress, 3rd Section, 1878)

Fowler, Arlen L. *The Black Infantry in the West, 1869-1891* (Norman, OK: University of Oklahoma Press, 1996)

Hershler, N. *The Soldier's Hand-Book for the Use of the Enlisted Men of the Army* (Washington, DC: Government Printing Office, 1889)

Jamieson, Perry D. *Crossing the Deadly Ground: United States Army Tactics, 1865–1899* (Tuscaloosa, AL: The University of Alabama Press, 1994)

Knight, Oliver *Life and Manners in the Frontier Army* (Norman, OK: University of Oklahoma Press, 1978)

McChristian, Douglas C. *The U.S. Army in the West, 1870–1880* (Norman, OK: University of Oklahoma Press, 1995)

Mahon, John K. and Romana, Danysh *Infantry Part I: Regular Army* (Washington, DC: Office of the Chief of Military History, 1972)

Powell, William H. *The Army Officer's Examiner* (New York: John Wiley & Sons, 1894)

Rickey, Don *Forty Miles a Day on Beans and Hay* (Norman, OK: University of Oklahoma Press, 1963)

Roberts, Larry Don *The Artillery with the Regular Army in the West from 1866 to 1890* (Ph.D. dissertation, Oklahoma State University, 1981)

Rodenbough, Theophilus F. and Haskin, William L. *The Army of the United States* (New York: Maynard, Merrill & Co., 1896)

Smith, Thomas T. *The Old Army in Texas* (Austin, TX: Texas State Historical Association, 2000)

Steffen, Randy *The Horse Soldier 1776–1943, Volume II: the Frontier, the Mexican War, the Civil War, the Indian War 1851–1880* (Norman, OK: University of Oklahoma Press, 1978)

Upton, Emory *Infantry Tactics Single and Double Ranks* (New York, NY: D. Appleton & Co., 1877)

Urwin, Gregory J.W. *The United States Cavalry* (Poole: Blanford, 1983)

Urwin, Gregory J.W. *The United States Infantry* (New York, NY: Sterling Press, 1991)

Utley, Robert M. *Frontier Regulars 1866–1891* (Lincoln, NE: University of Nebraska Press, 1973)

Wagner, Arthur L. *Organization and Tactics* (New York, NY: B. Westermann & Co., 1895)

War Department *Artillery Tactics* (New York: D. Appleton & Co., 1874)

War Department *Cavalry Tactics* (New York: D. Appleton & Co., 1874)

War Department *Regulations of the Army of the United States* (Washington, DC: Government Printing Office, 1881)

War Department *Report of the Secretary of War* (Washington, DC: Government Printing Office, various volumes 1865–91)

War Department *Revised Regulations of the Army of the United States* (Philadelphia, PA: J.B. Lippincott & Co., 1861)

Weigley, Russell F. *History of the United States Army, Enlarged Edition* (Indiana University Press, 1984)

Wooster, Robert *The Military and United States Indian Policy 1865–1903* (New Haven, CT: Yale University Press, 1988)

Index

Figures in **bold** refer to illustrations